Narrative Therapy
and Older People

also by this author

Life Story Work with People with Dementia
Ordinary Lives, Extraordinary People
Edited by Polly Kaiser and Ruth Eley
ISBN 978 1 84905 505 5
eISBN 978 0 85700 914 2

of related interest

Health Equality and Social Justice in Old Age
A Frontline Perspective
Dr Riaz Dharamshi
ISBN 978 1 83997 365 9
eISBN 978 1 83997 381 9

Why Dementia Makes Communication Difficult
A Guide to Better Outcomes
Alison Wray
ISBN 978 1 78775 606 9
eISBN 978 1 78775 607 6

Working Within Diversity
A Reflective Guide to Anti-Oppressive Practice in Counselling and Therapy
Myira Khan
ISBN 978 1 83997 098 6
eISBN 978 1 83997 099 3

Counselling and Psychotherapy with Older People in Care
A Support Guide
Felicity Chapman
ISBN 978 1 78592 396 8
eISBN 978 1 78450 751 0

Narrative Therapy and Older People

Challenging Stigma, Supporting Connection and Building Hope

EDITED BY
Rosslyn Offord, Elizabeth Field and Polly Kaiser

FOREWORDS BY DR RICHARD CHESTON AND HUGH FOX

Jessica Kingsley Publishers
London and Philadelphia

First published in Great Britain in 2026 by Jessica Kingsley Publishers
An imprint of John Murray Press

1

Copyright © Forewords: Dr Richard Cheston and Hugh Fox 2026
Chapter 1: Rosslyn Offord, Elizabeth Field and Polly Kaiser 2026
Chapter 2: Becky Scullion and Rosslyn Offord 2026
Chapter 3: Sara Banks, Pete Ord, Polly Kaiser and Rosslyn Offord 2026
Chapter 4: Polly Kaiser, Daniel Blake and Jane Grant 2026
Chapter 5: Rosslyn Offord, Jane Grant and Polly Kaiser 2026
Chapter 6: Rosslyn Offord and Karen Gibbs 2026
Chapter 7: Helen Carter 2026
Chapter 8: Elizabeth Field, Liz Jennings and Chris Norris 2026
Chapter 9: Gemma Barry and Elizabeth Field 2026
Chapter 10: Diane Clare 2026
Afterword: Polly Kaiser, Rosslyn Offord and Elizabeth Field 2026

The right of the above named authors to be identified as the Author of the Work has been asserted by them in accordance with the Copyright, Designs and Patents Act 1988.

Front cover image source: Adobe Stock. The cover image is for illustrative purposes only, and any person featuring is a model.

All rights reserved. No part of this publication may be reproduced, stored in a retrieval system, or transmitted, in any form or by any means without the prior written permission of the publisher, nor be otherwise circulated in any form of binding or cover other than that in which it is published and without a similar condition being imposed on the subsequent purchaser.

A CIP catalogue record for this title is available from the
British Library and the Library of Congress

ISBN 978 1 80501 242 9
eISBN 978 1 80501 243 6

Printed and bound by CPI Group (UK) Ltd, Croydon, CR0 4YY

Jessica Kingsley Publishers' policy is to use papers that are natural, renewable and recyclable products and made from wood grown in sustainable forests. The logging and manufacturing processes are expected to conform to the environmental regulations of the country of origin.

Jessica Kingsley Publishers
Carmelite House
50 Victoria Embankment
London EC4Y 0DZ

www.jkp.com

John Murray Press
Part of Hodder & Stoughton Ltd
An Hachette Company

The authorised representative in the EEA is Hachette Ireland,
8 Castlecourt Centre, Dublin 15, D15 XTP3, Ireland (email: info@hbgi.ie)

Contents

BIOGRAPHIES 7

FOREWORD BY DR RICHARD CHESTON 11

FOREWORD BY HUGH FOX 13

1. Introduction and Welcome 15
   Rosslyn Offord, Elizabeth Field and Polly Kaiser

2. What is Narrative Therapy? A Deeper Dive. 25
   Becky Scullion and Rosslyn Offord with contributions from Sara Banks and Pete Ord

3. Discourses: The Stories That Shape Us 41
   Sara Banks, Pete Ord, Polly Kaiser and Rosslyn Offord

4. 'Like the Voice of a Bird Singing in the Rain, Let Grateful Memory Survive in the Hour of Darkness': Using Narrative Practices to Scaffold Helpful Conversations about Loss and Dying 61
   Polly Kaiser, Daniel Blake and Jane Grant

5. Using Narrative Therapy with Older People Who Have Experienced Trauma: Strengthening Stories of Resistance and Giving Voice to What is Precious 79
   Rosslyn Offord, Jane Grant and Polly Kaiser with contributions from Vivienne Lowe and Becky Scullion

6. What Does It Feel Like to Experience Narrative Therapy? Using Narrative Therapy to Help Navigate the Journey in Becoming a Dementia Care Partner 95
   Rosslyn Offord and Karen Gibbs

7. Working Alongside Service Users with Narrative Therapy Practices. 109
   Helen Carter

8. Out of Therapy and into Life: Working with Groups and Communities. 125
   Elizabeth Field, Liz Jennings and Chris Norris with contributions from Polly Kaiser and Asesha Morjaria-Keval

9. Supporting Colleagues: Holding onto Hope and Connection 149
   Gemma Barry and Elizabeth Field with contributions from Jane Grant, Polly Kaiser, Asesha Morjaria-Keval, Rosslyn Offord and Becky Scullion

10. Ageing as Therapists: Acknowledging Our Ancestors and Leaving a Legacy 167
    Diane Clare with contributions from Polly Kaiser, Rosslyn Offord and Elizabeth Field

    AFTERWORD. 181
    Polly Kaiser, Rosslyn Offord and Elizabeth Field

    REFERENCES 187

    SUBJECT INDEX 195

    AUTHOR INDEX 201

Biographies

Rosslyn Offord is a clinical psychologist and narrative therapist, who grew up in Nottingham but moved to Wales to attend university in Cardiff. She did her clinical psychology training in Sheffield, where she had the privilege to meet some brilliant older adult psychologists, who inspired her to work with older people. After qualifying she returned to the coast of South Wales, where she has lived and worked with older people for over 20 years, specialising in dementia, for which she is the clinical psychology lead for Cardiff and the Vale of Glamorgan. Rosslyn has been active in pursuing her passion for narrative therapy and bringing together people who share this interest. She was awarded the Bill Downes Award by the British Psychological Society's (BPS) Faculty of Psychology of Older People in 2024 for her work in promoting narrative therapy and her commitment to the psychological care of older people in Wales and the Welsh language, which she has been learning over many years. Outside of work, Rosslyn loves to swim in the sea, walk the coastal paths and play in a local orchestra.

Elizabeth Field has enjoyed the company of older people and learning social history since she was young. She is a clinical psychologist with a diploma in narrative therapy who has worked with older people in the NHS for over 25 years and is now the lead for psychological practice in East Kent, and Kent lead for older people's psychological services in her NHS trust. She teaches, writes and uses narrative practices in her work with staff, trainees, patients and community groups. She leads on her trust's award-winning work engaging with people with dementia to challenge stigma, improve health and community services and promote the arts and well-being. Outside of work, Elizabeth enjoys crafting, exploring the countryside by tandem and her community involvement.

Polly Kaiser is a semi-retired clinical psychologist who has worked with older people and their carers since 1984; first, as a researcher in England and France, and then as a clinical psychologist in the north-west of England. She was the national lead for mental health in later life at the Department of Health (2009–2011) National Mental Health Development Unit and has been a long-term committee member of the BPS Faculty of Psychology of Older People. She has run workshops on a variety of topics including ageing awareness, diversity and ageing, sexuality and ageing, and bereavement. Currently she supports Greater Manchester Mature Minds Matters, a group of older people with lived experience advising the Greater Manchester NHS and wider Greater Manchester ageing initiatives. Polly loves being outdoors, singing and eating, not necessarily all at the same time. She has always been a champion of age equality and now, as an older woman herself, has skin in the game.

Sara Banks worked for many years with colleagues to support older people with stroke and neurological conditions in acute and neuro-rehabilitation services. She now works in the NHS, with older people coming to see her via mental health and memory services, and for Queen Mary University London, undertaking funded research into older people's experience of eating disorders and food addiction.

Gemma Barry is a clinical psychologist who lived and worked in a community dementia team in South Wales for a number of years post-qualification. Her main role was supporting individuals living with young onset dementia and their family members. She has recently moved back to London where she works in a memory team.

Daniel Blake is a clinical psychologist, systemic psychotherapist and supervisor in South-West Yorkshire Partnership Trust. His early interest in narrative practices drew him to a final year specialist placement with Polly where they introduced narrative and systemic ideas. He has since continued his development in narrative practices via his further training and clinical practice. He works with older adult teams and family clinics and provides supervision and training.

Helen Carter is a clinical psychologist and narrative therapist who has worked for over 20 years in the south-west of England. She enjoys applying narrative practices to any situation, but this is predominantly in her NHS work with older people and with staff teams.

Diane Clare is a consultant clinical psychologist – born in London and later emigrating to New Zealand in 1981 where she completed her training as a psychotherapist, including narrative therapy, before becoming a clinical psychologist. Working in the UK and in New Zealand across the adult age range, including older adults, she is a specialist in trauma and a Fellow of the International Society for the Study of Trauma and Dissociation.

Karen Gibbs was married for 40 years to Nick and spent the last 10 of those years supporting him through the challenges of young onset dementia until he died at the age of 64. Together with her husband, she enjoyed a stable marriage and a happy family life bringing up three loving daughters. She is now fortunate to have two young granddaughters too. While Nick pursued a career in marketing and business management, Karen worked for many years as a teacher of German and French. She loves cooking, sewing and knitting, participates in regular ballroom and Latin dance classes and attends weekly yoga sessions. She lives with her cat in Penarth, South Wales.

Jane Grant is a clinical psychologist and has worked in Yorkshire within older people's community mental health and memory services for over 15 years. Narrative therapy has been a big part of what has inspired and sustained her work over this time.

Liz Jennings is an author and creative group facilitator who loves encouraging others in their creativity and seeing the ways the arts connect people with each other and themselves. She developed her first writing group with people with dementia in partnership with Keith

Oliver in 2014. Since then, her groups have involved life writing, play and film writing and poetry, and she has edited two collections of writing by people with dementia, *Welcome to Our World* and *Time and Place*.

Vivienne Lowe sadly died on New Year's Eve 2024, just after the final draft of this book was completed. She was excited to contribute to what she viewed as an important project, which she saw as providing hope to people like her who had come through difficult times. Viv leaves behind her a devoted partner, daughter and grand daughter, and a wide circle of friends and family. She lived bravely, generously and joyfully and is greatly missed.

Asesha Morjaria-Keval is a consultant clinical psychologist and has worked within older people's community and inpatient mental health services across Kent and Medway for over 12 years. She is now the head of service for older people's psychological services in the Highlands, Scotland, where she has begun to introduce narrative practices in therapy, supervision and with teams.

Chris Norris lives in Kent and was diagnosed with frontotemporal dementia in December 2012. He is a dementia envoy for Kent and Medway NHS Mental Health Trust. He works hard to fight the stigma around dementia and to create better understanding about the condition. In his working life, he was a musician in the army, a village policeman and a driving examiner, among other occupations.

Pete Ord is a clinical psychologist currently working in mental health services for the NHS near London, exploring ways of using narrative practices to support men admitted to a psychiatric intensive care unit.

Becky Scullion is a clinical psychologist and has worked within NHS services for over 13 years. She works within a community mental health service for older people in the south-east of England and is committed to integrating aspects of narrative practice throughout all aspects of her work.

Foreword

This is a book about the stories that we tell ourselves and why understanding how these stories frame our lives is important.

So much of our world is made up of voices telling us different stories. These stories may be handed down to us from our parents, much like a weathered coat – comforting in their nostalgia, but patchy and perhaps not as helpful as they used to be. Or they could leap out at us from phones that are full of lifestyle hacks and unfeasibly alluring promises. Or maybe the stories are those that our peers and acquaintances tell us – where the narratives are casually edited to position the teller as the hero or the victim in a daily struggle with life's chaos.

These different stories tell us about who we are, how we should be and what we should aspire to – they are stories that define the sort of person that we should be and what our relationship should be with the major, existential themes in our lives – our ageing, mortality and illness.

As this book sets out so well, we weave these stories into our lives – they help us to make sense out of who we are and what we are to become. Should we be a brave battler whistling our way into eternity or a wise guru, comfortably grounded in our lives? Or should we, like Jenny Joseph, choose between a sudden desire to wear purple with a red hat that doesn't suit or instead continue wearing dry, sensible clothes and avoid swearing in the street?

The stories we hear, and those we tell ourselves about the sort of person we should be, are the contexts within which therapy – and indeed so much more – takes place. As Lynn Hoffman has suggested, as therapists we often take on the role of a friendly editor in our clients' lives, helping them to reconstruct and reframe their narratives.

This book takes the form of a series of multilayered conversations between the authors and the reader, with chapters including tips for practice and reflection points offering alternative perspectives and voices. At the same time, there are also conversations between authors – a choir of voices commenting and reflecting on these ideas.

Reading this book introduced me to new ways of thinking about my own therapeutic practice and helped me to make sense of the things many clients had described to me. But at the same time, this is much more than just a book for psychotherapists working with older adults. It will guide any healthcare worker who wants to understand more about the distress in the people that they work with.

Perhaps most importantly of all, this book will speak to anyone with an interest in what it is to grow old – especially if this is about their own ageing. Thus, while I wish that I had been able to read this book at the start of my career, I'm just grateful that I have encountered it as I struggle (like a number of the book's authors) to peel back the curtain on how I can shape my life beyond retirement.

Whatever interest has brought you to this book, I am sure you will find reading it a rich and rewarding experience.

Dr Richard Cheston, School of Social Sciences,
University of the West of England, Bristol

Foreword

This book fills an important gap in the literature of narrative therapy, and I'm sure also in the literature of working with older people. I enthusiastically recommend it to anyone who works with older people or, indeed, who knows any older people. It is accessible, engaging and full of good ideas: once I started reading it I found it hard to put down!

Full disclosure: I have known Rosslyn Offord, Elizabeth Field and Polly Kaiser for many years as colleagues or students/ex-students. I am delighted that they have worked, together with a community of other folk (with many of whom I also have connections), to write about this subject.

I was immediately drawn in by the open and welcoming tone of the first chapter and its emphasis on standing against stigma, stereotype and injustice. This appeared to be a book for me, an activist book written in a spirit of resistance!

The book goes on to cover a wide range of topics relating narrative ideas and practices to working with older people. It also has sections on working alongside carers, on working with groups and communities as well as on supporting others who do this work. Different voices are introduced throughout the book, including the voices of service users and their carers. There are small nuggets of narrative ideas clearly separated off in boxes so that they can be digested separately; there are questions for reflection; and there are lots of practice examples.

This is an important contribution to the conversation about working with older people. One of the most refreshing aspects of this work is the way it helps to shift the discourse from one where older people are the subjects of the professional gaze to one where their voices and wishes are centred.

This is a must-read for all who work in this field and also for everyone who teaches those who will work in this field in the future.

As a person who has been teaching narrative for over a quarter of a century, it is deeply gratifying to see how these ideas are influencing the future of work in this area. Thank you, Rosslyn, Elizabeth and Polly!

Hugh Fox, Institute of Narrative Therapy

CHAPTER 1

Introduction and Welcome

Rosslyn Offord, Elizabeth Field and Polly Kaiser

Hello and thank you for joining us in thinking together about narrative therapy and working with older people and people living with dementia. We are very pleased that you have joined us. Our hope is that the chapters which follow will have the feel of a conversation – between us and with you. We're keen to share our understanding of the joys of narrative therapy and narrative practice and how it can assist older people in managing challenges and joining together. We would like this conversation to grow beyond this book and would love to hear from others who are working in similar ways. You will find signposts to further reading and resources throughout the book and contact details at the end.

Most contributors are fully named, but where people wanted to be anonymised we have changed their details to the degree they wanted. In historic cases where we have not been able to gain permission, we have anonymised substantially so people are no longer identifiable.

A note on terminology: narrative therapy and narrative practice

Before we continue, we will clarify something about the terms 'narrative therapy' and 'narrative practice'. We will use 'narrative therapy' to refer to the specific type of therapy, based on narrative principles, which may be used in a clinical or therapeutic setting. We will share examples of using narrative therapy with people who have been referred to mental health or dementia services for psychological therapy to help manage their distress. 'Narrative practice' is a broader umbrella term within which narrative therapy sits. When we are talking about narrative practice, we are referring to broader ways of working, such as ways of supporting staff teams or community groups.

Introductions: who we are and why we are here

Before we go further, we would like to say a little bit about who we are. We, Rosslyn, Polly and Elizabeth, who have edited this book, along with most of our authors, are people who are trained as clinical psychologists and have gone on to do training in narrative therapy. It's important to say that you absolutely don't have to be a psychologist to be a narrative therapist or to use narrative ideas, as you'll see from Liz Jennings in Chapter 8, who is a writer and creative group facilitator. As a group, we have come to know each other through the Institute of Narrative Therapy and the British Psychological Society's Faculty of Psychologists Working with Older People. In writing some of these chapters, we have been joined by co-authors, including people who have consulted us as users of services where we work, including Vivienne Lowe in Chapter 5, Karen Gibbs in Chapter 6 and Chris Norris in Chapter 8. They will introduce themselves as we go along.

As psychologists we all work, or have worked, for the National Health Service (NHS) in the UK. Between us, we work across services in Wales, Scotland, England and Aotearoa New Zealand, some of us in community mental health teams, some in dementia services, others in hospitals and some in the private and charity sectors. We are at a range of life and career stages: Polly and Diane are recently retired; Gemma and Dan are in the early stages of their careers. The rest of us are somewhere in the middle. As a group of authors, we come from different social and ethnic backgrounds although most (but not all) of us are women, and most (but not all) of us are White. Most, but not all, of us are heterosexual and all identify with the gender we were assigned at birth. We range in age from our early 30s through to our late 70s. Some of us have children, some of us don't. Some of us are monoglots, some of us speak other languages. Many of us were born into working-class homes and were the first in our families to go to university; some of us were born into more affluent, middle-class families. Some of us hold religious beliefs, others do not. We share this with you to help you picture us and to help you understand our roots. This is important as we have come to understand how the life experiences and the groups we are a part of shape the way we experience the world and the way we see things. As editors, the three of us acknowledge the privilege we hold, both as White people and as senior professional people with the fancy job title of 'consultant clinical psychologist'. Recognising the way these factors shape our experience of the world relates to a fundamental part of narrative practice – our identities and what is important to us are shaped by the people around us and the experiences we have living in this time and place.

This book emerges from a friendship between Rosslyn and Elizabeth, who first met on a narrative therapy training course in London back in the early 2000s. They were drawn to each other as the only participants working with older people. Over the following years at further narrative training, they started to find other older adult psychologists and recognised the gap there seemed to be in narrative writing and training pertinent to working with older people. Rosslyn proposed an online coming together with the idea of writing a book and approached Polly for help, as a trusted older colleague with experience in book writing! Sadly, not all our authors could be with us; however, in July 2023, the three of us had the pleasure of joining with Helen, Gemma, Jane, Becky and Sara in Manchester, England, to develop the basis of this book. This chapter is based on our initial conversation, in which we used the Tree of Life (of which you will find more in Chapters 8 and 9) to draw out the connections between us and what we want to say about why narrative therapy is important to us in our work with older people. This is what emerged.

The appeal of working with people who are older

We have noticed how the ageism we see in the wider world comes into our health and social care services. We see the stigma and the stereotypes that create misconceptions and difficulties for us in recruiting staff; we also see the relative lack of funding for services used by older people, such as in mental healthcare. For some of us this sense of injustice was the very thing that drew us into this work!

Many of us came to work in psychology and in the NHS with a commitment to social justice, and were outraged to discover how little the needs of older people can appear to be valued. For all of us this rubbed up against our own experience of older people, who have been important and influential in our own lives. Some of us were attracted by the feistiness and outspokenness of our psychology leaders in this field, who modelled a way of working that spoke out and stood up for older people. This was a big factor for Rosslyn, for example. She had seen the discrepancy between how services appeared to see her grandfather, where he seemed to be defined in terms of his physical frailty and his dementia, without recognition of the man he had been and continued to be: a respected member of his community; a man who had lived and survived decades of social change and challenge; a proud Ulster and Irish man; a lover of Irish culture, whiskey and football; a cheerleader for his granddaughters. Meeting psychologists soon after his death who advocated for the rights of older people and championed person-centred ways of working was therefore highly significant to her.

As a group we shared the sense of privilege in listening to people's stories. It is probably obvious to say that people who have lived longer lives have far more stories to tell! And it can feel more interesting to hear about lives lived in different and changing times. As Elizabeth's daughter said, 'so much more has happened'. We have learned so much about the history of our own and other countries from the stories that have been shared with us. As examples of this, Elizabeth listed subjects as diverse as Persian poetry, partition in India, Polish ghettos in the Second World War, filmmaking, animal conservation and farm vehicle maintenance! A favourite story for her was learning from several people in the same town how, as young people, they had been told that teenage sex would cause dementia!

As a group we shared how people often say things like, 'Your job must be very depressing,' and marvelled at this common misconception! On the contrary, we have been humbled and inspired to witness how adaptable and creative many people are in travelling through life. As Polly pointed out, the fact that people have made it to later life speaks to the capacity and resourcefulness that those who consult us have to teach us. We have also been taught and reminded about what matters in life.

Narrative practice is collaborative: the therapist is not the expert; the older person is in the driving seat

The first thing that our group of writers said, when we discussed why we were drawn to narrative approaches, was its 'non-expert' way of thinking: the people who access our support are the experts in their lives, not us as workers (Morgan 2000). We are asked to put aside our assumptions and theories about other people's lives and instead invite a way of talking that enables us to collaborate in finding a different way to approach the difficulties people bring to us. This can feel very different to other psychotherapeutic approaches, in which we are invited to hold expertise and guide or advise people. For Helen, this non-expert position in narrative therapy, where we try to place the person we work with, not ourselves, at the centre fits well, known as 'de-centred' practice in narrative therapy. As she put it, 'It's easy to be de-centred in working with older people because we are (mostly!) the youngest and will therefore be educated by virtue of being the less experienced person in the room'. Or, as Polly put it, 'You can't pull the wool over older people's eyes!'

The ideas and tools that narrative therapy gives us to honour this principle are highly valued by us all. Elizabeth appreciates the way that the onus is on the therapist to scaffold questions, so that people are able to answer them and learn new things about themselves; people do not need to be literate, articulate or have a good memory to benefit from a narrative therapy conversation. Sara said, 'The way in which serious problems can be approached in a playful manner is something that keeps me coming to work. I find that the people who come to see me, particularly, are surprised by what this can offer – it's a pleasure to be able to find the fun when times are tough'.

Understanding older people's lives in their cultural, social and political context

Our experiences have led us to understand how far people's life experiences are shaped by the cultural, social and political context in which they live. Narrative therapy is an approach that recognises and values the different perspectives people may hold and pays attention to how these are shaped by someone's context – their family, their friends, their community and so on. The theoretical underpinnings of this are explained more in Chapter 2. As narrative therapists we invite people to explain this for us. It helps us to step aside from some of the practices of psychological therapy, which have been criticised for assumptions they carry based on ideas that come from European and American traditions (e.g. Owusu-Bempah and Howitt 2000). With this in mind, we want to acknowledge the inevitable limitations of this book. We can only speak to our experience of using these approaches in the UK and Aotearoa New Zealand and from the perspectives we bring in relation to our own genders, ethnicities, ages and so on. Throughout the book we will share references to examples of narrative practice in other cultures. It did after all originate in Australia and Aotearoa New Zealand, not the UK, and some of the practices we share were developed in other parts of the world, such as Tree of Life, referenced in Chapters 8 and 9, which was developed in Southern Africa by Ncube (2006). We invite you to consider how well or not the practices we share would fit for you within the context you work and what may need adapting.

Understanding people in context also calls us to consider the effects of inequality and discrimination, and narrative therapy provides tools to assist us with this. Indeed, narrative therapy was born out of White and Epston's (2009) awareness and discomfort about the various forms of inequality they witnessed. This included the injustices associated with the marginalisation of indigenous knowledge and culture (C. White 2009). Arulampalam et al. (2006) have discussed a psychological colonisation of people's lives, in addition to the historical physical colonisation of indigenous communities. White and Epston's discomfort with this influenced their ideas. They saw narrative therapy as a form of social justice and an ethical way of responding (C. White 2009). In our working lives, many of us have found other psychological therapies lacking in this way; even when factors such as prejudice or poverty are acknowledged, the focus has primarily been on internal thoughts and feelings. As explained by Smail (1978, 2005), there can be a risk in inadvertently blaming people for their problems if their social and environmental pressures are not addressed. We are drawn to narrative practice as it helps us to find creative ways to both acknowledge and challenge these issues in our therapeutic work and to share ideas that work with groups and communities. Polly, for example, joined with mental-health community development workers Abdul Shakoor, John Newton, Shaista Nazir and Atifa Liaqat to work with older South Asian women to address difficulties of stigma and prejudice in accessing mental health services, using narrative practices in a project called Making Connections, Not Assumptions. Sharing stories of migration and identity led to the co-production of a mental health awareness campaign.

Narrative therapy is recognised as an approach that is consistent with the values of a more 'trauma-informed' approach, fundamental to which is the recognition of what people have been through in their lives, with an emphasis on 'What has happened to you?' rather than 'What is wrong with you?' (Boyle and Johnstone 2020; Johnstone et al. 2018). This was an aspect of narrative therapy that drew in Polly, whose reading of Ryan's (1976) book *Blaming the Victim* had been pivotal to her, and Rosslyn, who had spent her teens wearing a badge bearing R.D. Laing's famous quote, 'Do not adjust your mind, the fault is in reality' (Laing 1978)!

Working in solidarity: we are all part of the same humanity

Some further ideas that have resonated for us have been around building solidarity in response to challenge or oppression. Asesha was drawn to this aspect of the approach, which is addressed particularly in the work of David Denborough (2008). Discovering ideas for using collective practices, which enable people to connect together in their shared challenges, inspired her work with people living with dementia, as described along with other collective practices in Chapter 9. For Rosslyn, these ideas resonated with the work of Tom Kitwood, a psychologist with a specialism in dementia care, who wrote about the importance of the social environment and said, we are all part of the same humanity (Kitwood 1997).

Throughout the book we will share ways in which we have tried to come alongside and collaborate with the people we work with. In particular, we refer you to Chapter 7, in which Helen shares how she has collaborated with users of mental health services to support others, and Chapter 8, where a range of collective narrative practices with community groups are shared. You will also see that several chapters are co-written with people with whom we have worked. In Chapter 5, Viv shares her experience of using narrative therapy to overcome some of the effects of trauma; in Chapter 6, Karen shares her experience as a carer for her husband, and in Chapter 8, Chris shares the impact of being involved in a Tree of Life group. The many ways in which narrative practice has informed the ways we have found to support and collaborate with our colleagues also speaks to solidarity and will be shared by Gemma and others in Chapter 9.

When writing about the people who use our services or consult us, we have used the term 'service user', as we have found that this tends to be the preferred term. However, we acknowledge that not everyone likes or uses this terminology; one day we hope a new term will emerge with a better consensus!

A focus on strengths and personal agency

Narrative therapy recognises how frequently people who have experienced trauma lose the sense of agency or ability to have some control in their lives (e.g. White 2006). In contrast, narrative therapy seeks to put service users in the 'driving seat'. Asking the person for permission to ask certain questions and giving them a choice in the direction of the conversation are important ways in which we can create a different experience for older people who consult us. We often see how the experience of dementia, and/or physical or mental health challenges, can lead to a lack of choice or control. Narrative therapy has chimed well for us, with an emphasis on drawing out skills, abilities and intentions and making these more visible to the people we work with, who may often have lost sight of these. This way of working is visible in all of the work we describe but is emphasised particularly in Chapter 3, where we look at the stories that shape us; in Chapter 4, where Polly, Jane and Dan discuss working with grief and loss; and in Chapter 5, where Rosslyn, Jane, Polly, Viv and Becky consider how these ideas can be of assistance in supporting people to overcome the effects of trauma on their lives. You will also find uplifting examples of work that shares stories of strength and ability in Chapter 8.

Readers interested in person-centred care will recognise how acknowledging people's strengths and abilities is an important component of dignity. This is well documented in both mental health and dementia care. We hear from older people how often they feel that opportunities to make a contribution or to help others are denied to them, and they can feel as if they are constantly in the role of relying on others or needing help. Community psychologists have long recognised the importance of being part of not just social networks, but also social action, in which you have something to give as well as receive (e.g. Holland 1992). You can read examples of this in Chapter 8, where people take actions to challenge stigma, assumptions and stereotypes about ageing and dementia.

Challenging stigma and 'discourses'

When we consider stigma and stereotypes about ageing, it has helped us to understand the concept of 'discourses'. This refers to the kinds of expectations that we are subjected to, based on things like our age, gender ethnicity and so on, as Sara and Pete will explain and illustrate in Chapter 3. In Chapter 6, Karen talks about how expectations about retirement affected how she felt about the way she lived her life as a dementia carer. In Chapter 10, we hear from Diane and Polly about discourses around retirement, and in Chapter 8, Chris and others talk about how they challenge the stigma that impacts them, resulting from particular discourses around dementia.

Some suggestions about how to approach the book

We hope we have been able to give you a sense of what is to come. We invite those of you who want to understand more about the theory and technical aspects of the approach to continue to Chapter 2. We will include some theory in later chapters as we go along. We will do our best to illustrate these theories through the stories and examples we share, which we hope you may connect with and find useful. At times, there is additional detail about theory or specifics about exercises or strategies that may be of interest to some readers, like those of you who are therapists or academics. In these cases, we have separated out the details into text boxes, so that you can consult them without it interrupting the flow for everyone else.

For those of you who are keen to understand more about social discourses, or 'prescriptions for living', we suggest Chapter 3. Chapters 4 and 5 will take you through examples of working within the contexts of grief and loss and trauma. Chapter 6 will help you understand more about how it feels to experience narrative therapy as both a service user and as a therapist, as well as some insights into the experiences of being a dementia care giver. Chapter 7 shares outsider witness practices and collaborating with service users in therapy, while Chapter 8 takes us out of the therapy room and into community working. Chapter 9 will be useful for those interested in ways of using narrative practice to support colleagues, while Chapter 10 provides a perspective on ageing as a therapist.

Each chapter stands alone, although you will see references to other chapters where we might signpost you to find out more about a particular approach. Chapter 2 is designed as a kind of glossary of ideas to help with this. Do feel free to skip the detail in text boxes if it isn't of interest to you; the writing is designed to work without these parts. Finally, if it's helpful, take the time to consider the 'invitations to reflect' that we include, which aim to include you as an active part of this conversation. We include recommendations for further reading and resources for each chapter for those who want to learn more or seek other perspectives.

We hope you enjoy your journey with us.

CHAPTER 2

What is Narrative Therapy? A Deeper Dive

Becky Scullion and Rosslyn Offord
with contributions from Sara Banks and Pete Ord

In Chapter 1, we have attempted to introduce you to some of the key ideas or principles that we understand to underpin narrative practice. This chapter is written for those of you who are interested in knowing more about the roots of these ideas, the background theory and the technical details of some of the main aspects of narrative practice to provide some context to the stories we go on to share in later chapters. As with all the chapters in this book, our hope is that this chapter can stand alone and be complete in itself. However, it is also written as a kind of glossary, so that you can refer back to it if you need to check out particular ideas or concepts. As we mention in Chapter 1, we have separated out more technical parts into text boxes, which can easily be skipped if they feel less relevant to you.

In trying to explain and describe narrative therapy, we immediately run into some challenges. We share the following quote from David Epston and Michael White (cited in Beels 2009, p.363), to illustrate this:

> We have been steadfast in our refusal to name our work in any consistent manner...We believe that such a naming would only subtract from our freedom to further explore various ideas and practices, and that it would make it difficult for others to recognise their own unique contributions to developments in this work, which we regard to be an 'open book'. We are drawing attention to the fact that one of the aspects

associated with this work that is of central importance to us is the spirit of adventure.

As this highlights, and as Beels (2009) helps us to understand, David Epston and Michael White distanced themselves from the centre of the new movement that has since been named narrative therapy. For Cheryl White (2009), what stood out for her in relation to the ideas that Epston and White co-produced was a 'joy in offering them out to a world that was looking for new ways of working' (p.59), as opposed to an ownership of ideas. In this book, we are keen to reflect the 'spirit of adventure' that White and Epston set out to preserve throughout their work. We hope that our writing will, in turn, be an invitation for additional exploration and encourage the co-evolution of further ideas in ways that, as White and Epston hoped, would be 'enriching…to the lives of those persons who seek our help' (cited in C. White 2009, p.59). Although we will pick out and attempt to explain some of these ideas, we want to acknowledge that, in doing so, there will be many other definitions/stories and experiences that will be missed. We encourage you to remain adventurous in your reading, to seek diversity and to maintain the sense of the 'open book' nature of this wonderful form of therapy that White and Epston held close to them.

What do we understand as being the roots of narrative therapy?

This 'spirit of adventure' began in the late 1970s, when White and Epston first started having conversations with each other (C. White 2009). It is understood that many of the ideas they developed together have their foundations in social constructionism. This approach, as described by Burr (2003), insists that we question our 'taken-for-granted' ways of understanding the world. This includes questioning ourselves and the origins of our own beliefs. As described by Hoffman (1990), social construction theory holds that our beliefs about the world and the development of knowledge are social inventions that are created and developed in conversation with other people. Knowledge will therefore look different at different points in time or across different cultures. This knowledge can be seen as a collection of 'truths' we all hold about the world. These 'truths' shape how we behave towards one another and how we compare ourselves to others.

At points in this chapter, we will introduce you to Maeve, an Irish woman in her late 70s. Maeve's story was shared with us by Sara, who was asked to offer psychological therapy to her for a 'depressive episode' experienced following a number of recent bereavements. We hope that examples from Maeve's story will help to illustrate the ideas we are sharing here and bring them to life.

In considering the events in Maeve's life that had contributed to her distress, we can see how knowledge about the world has changed over time. In Maeve's case, her attempt to leave an abusive marriage was met with the response, 'You have made your bed'. To those not familiar with this phrase, it can follow with 'and now you must lie in it,' which means that once a decision is made you must stick to it. There is now a recognition in the UK and Ireland that domestic violence should not be tolerated, and it is now illegal. The knowledge that underpins this legislation is very different from the knowledge and understanding of the world held by Maeve's mother in Ireland back in the 1960s. In Maeve's case, this was accompanied by 'truths' about her duties as a wife and mother; being seen to 'fail' at these would be met with judgement, shame and stigma. Social constructionists emphasise the importance of language (Burr 2003) and power (Foucault 1980) in the construction of knowledge (Freedman and Combs 1996).

> In understanding how social constructionism differs from what Burr (2003) describes as 'traditional psychology', Burr points to a move away from the idea that people can be understood in terms of internal characteristics, such as personality traits or identities, which she describes as limiting. These 'traditional' ways of understanding people are often referred to as 'structuralist' ideas or principles. In comparison, therapies such as narrative therapy, along with systemic or family therapy, draw on social constructionism or 'poststructuralism/postmodernism'.

> For those interested in understanding more about how narrative therapy sits alongside family therapy, we refer you to Beels (2009) and Hayward (2009).

Narrative therapy, identity and power

Before we move on to consider the new and specific practices that emerged from the development of narrative therapy, it seems important to share some ideas around identity and power, which are important to the approach.

Identity

David Denborough (2009) helps us to understand how the ideas we have shared around how our identities are created in the context of our social environment are conceptualised in narrative therapy. Reflecting on Michael White's legacy, he writes how:

> Michael refused to locate the fears children were experiencing as in any way reflective of their 'inner character'. He refused to participate in internalising descriptions of problems. Instead, he believed there were good reasons why small children might be afraid in this culture. (Denborough, 2009, p.97)

In other words, his views were in stark contrast to structuralist thought which suggests that people have 'internal selves' and a 'core' where problems are located (Hayward 2009).

As Combs and Freedman (2016) highlight, these principles continue to evade the healthcare system, where systems are often pushed to diagnose people and assign labels to define their identities. This contrasts with a narrative understanding of identity as a 'relational, historically and culturally situated process that changes through time and context' (p.212). With this more fluid understanding of identity, therapy can assist in bringing forth different experiences of self and supporting people to choose what supports their preferred ways of being (Combs and Freedman 2016).

Power

When we talk about knowledge in narrative therapy we are also drawn to think about power. The origins of these ideas come from the French philosopher/theorist, Michel Foucault, whose ideas heavily influenced White and Epston (Besley 2002). Combs and Freedman (2004) explain how Foucault saw knowledge and power as interrelated. As we have seen, societal 'knowledge' is shaped by the historical and cultural context in which it is developed. Foucault described how the workings of power shift equally with shifts in knowledge (Combs and Freedman 2004). Foucault described two types of power: traditional power and modern power, where traditional power, as described by Combs and Freedman (2004) is 'that sort that we associate with kings and other patriarchs' (p.3), while modern power is more 'invisible…[and]…develops and circulates in widely dispersed and shifting communities' (p.3).

As therapists, we need to take account of how power is brokered within and beyond people's individual lives (Bostock 2017), and as Smail (2004) suggests, we need to understand how experiences of well-being and distress are linked with the operation of power. One way we can do this is to pay attention to the 'discourses', which are the social and cultural expectations which tell us how we should think, feel and behave, and which Sara and Pete will explain in Chapter 3. These kinds of pressures and expectations, such as how to be a good wife or how to age well, are understood as one way in which power is held by certain groups by putting down other groups. As an example, consider how pressures on older women to look younger lead many of us to spend money on beauty products, serving the interests of a multi-billion dollar industry.

As narrative therapists we can help people to notice these discourses operating in their lives and consider whether they are helpful to them or serve their interests. We have already seen how, in Maeve's case, social discourses about the duties of women of a Catholic faith, and of married women more generally, may have informed her mother's response when Maeve shared her plans to leave her husband. As with all of us, we are subject to many different discourses in our lives. Other discourses became apparent for Maeve when she considered how she had learned to feel she had to be in relationships: giving of herself, doing the looking after, sticking with commitments, making things work, putting herself last. Stepping back and considering the effects of these expectations was important to Maeve in making sense of her experience of what others regarded to be her 'low mood'. Hopefully, you can see how this would open up possibilities for Maeve that would not have emerged had she and Sara stuck with a narrower way of thinking about her experience that located her distress in a 'depressive episode' and a problem of her psychological make-up.

> **INVITATION TO REFLECT**
>
> - Are these ideas about society, identity and power familiar to you?
> - Does it make sense to you to consider these social ideas when thinking about psychological distress and therapy?

What this means in terms of practice

We will now move on to explore how the above ideas are expressed through some of the practices of narrative therapy. We cannot, of course, begin to do justice to the many and varied ways of practising that therapists have developed around the world, and which we encourage you to investigate. Here, we will attempt to share some of the ideas that are widely used by narrative therapists and explain practices that you will hear more about throughout this book.

Listening, 'being host' and 'de-centring'

Simply listening to the story someone tells us constitutes a revolutionary act. (Freedman and Combs 1996, p.44)

We will begin with the principle of *listening* from a narrative perspective. This is key in the context of storytelling and understanding the *meaning* behind the stories people tell us. This requires the therapist to approach listening without definitions of pathology (e.g. 'depressed' or 'paranoid') shaping how stories are heard and instead try to hear what has led the person to seek our assistance, in their language and from their perspective (Freedman and Combs 1996; Hoffman 1990). It is in this approach that narrative therapy can feel very different to other models of psychological therapy, where the expertise and knowledge of the therapist is placed at the centre and shapes the questions asked and the direction the session will take. (See Morgan 2000 for a fuller discussion of this.)

As highlighted in Chapter 1, the concept of de-centring is key to this, and can be understood as the giving away of 'expert' knowledge instead of privileging clients knowledge and skills. Freedman and Combs (1996) refer to this as the 'not-knowing' position. This does not mean that as therapists we completely let go of previous theory and knowledge, but we do try to be aware of how our training and our own experiences may cause us to make assumptions. In order to try and genuinely understand the perspective of the person speaking with us, we need to hold a position of not knowing and of curiosity. For Morgan (2000), it is the maintenance of a sense of curiosity and constantly asking questions to which the therapist genuinely does not know the answer that are the two most significant principles to inform narrative ways of working. For Aman (2006), the metaphor of the therapist as being a 'host' is a concept that she has drawn on to work some way towards addressing the power differentials in therapeutic relationships and putting de-centring into action. She emphasises the key role of transparency and collaboration in all aspects of her work.

'Thin' and 'thick' descriptions of stories and 'double listening'

When using the term 'story' within the context of narrative therapy, it is helpful to consider Morgan's (2000) definition of a story as consisting of:

- events
- linked in sequence
- across time
- according to a plot.

As Morgan (2000) explains, we seek to make meanings out of our experiences over time by weaving events together across a time frame to form the plot of the story. As this story develops, certain events that fit the developing plot get privileged over others and form what is referred to in narrative terms as the 'dominant plot'. As described by Morgan (2000), these may include 'thin descriptions' of people's actions and intentions, which are often decided by other people and leave little space for the complexities of life and alternative meanings. We can see an example of this in coming to label an older man as 'grumpy' or a woman as 'neurotic'. These thin descriptions can have devastating effects on how people come to think of themselves, their problem and their identity – for example, in perhaps thinking of themselves as a 'bad' person or 'hopeless'. As Morgan (2000, pp.13–14) describes, once thin conclusions take hold, 'It becomes very easy for people to engage in gathering evidence to support these dominant problem-saturated stories...and [can] lead to more thin conclusions as people's skills, knowledges, abilities and competencies become hidden by the problem story'.

In narrative therapy, we are guided by the belief that lives are multi-storied; in other words, many stories (both positive and negative) can occur at the same time. This means that when a 'dominant', 'problem-saturated' narrative takes hold, there are always alternative stories or plot lines available to be curious about. This is where our need to listen carefully and with curiosity becomes very important: we listen carefully so that we can try to hear the alternative stories that have become subsumed by the dominant story, and which might be preferred by the person or more useful to them. This type of careful listening out for alternatives is described as 'double listening' in narrative therapy (Guilfoyle 2015).

When we listen out for alternative stories, we might notice that something may be implied by what is said but not said directly. For example, someone may mention in passing that they check in on a neighbour on their way home from work. They may not think to say anything more about this choice but implicit in this action are other stories – perhaps values about caring for others, beliefs about civic responsibilities or maybe stories about an important relationship. We listen out for these details, which we refer to as 'absent but implicit'

(Carey, Walther and Russell 2009), as these may also point to alternative storylines about what is important to the person.

We aim to be curious in asking about these possible alternative stories and invite the person to talk more about them, if they feel that would be helpful. As explained by Morgan (2000), we invite this richer description of alternative stories in order to free people from the influence of problematic stories. In inviting more details about these preferred, alternative stories, they can then become more richly described or 'thickened'.

In this next section of the chapter, we will share some of the different types of conversations we can use in order to assist us in collaborating with older people to identify and thicken preferred, alternative storylines. The hope is that these approaches can lead to possibilities for new directions.

Maps as a metaphor

As White (2007) explains, his fascination with maps led him to use them as a metaphor for his conversations with the people who consulted him. Just as a map gives us various roads to enable us to reach our destination, so a 'map' for therapy gives us ideas for conversations (which may take various routes) that can be used to navigate an unexplored territory. White (2007, p.5) is keen to emphasise that these maps should not be considered as *the* maps of narrative practice but can offer means for therapists to respond to people in ways that 'open opportunities for them to explore neglected aspects of the territories of their own lives'.

The therapist provides scaffolding by asking incremental questions in such a way that the person is able to answer them, moving in gradual steps from the 'known and familiar' to an understanding of their identity that is 'possible to know' but previously not visible.

Externalising conversations: statement-of-position maps 1 and 2

In a moment, we will be sharing with you some example maps from Michael White to support you in having conversations. First, though, we want to draw your attention to a principle that underpins all of these conversations, and which White described as 'externalising' (White 1988/89). This comes from the social constructionist way of understanding distress that we shared earlier in the chapter. Narrative therapists do not see distress as located within a person or due to gaps or problems with their personality or development. Instead, problems are seen as arising out of complex social situations and as external to the person. Externalising is a way of asking about the problem in order to separate it from the person – 'in which the problem becomes the problem, not the person' (White 2007, p.26). As White (2007, p.26) writes, 'If a person's relationship with the problem becomes more clearly defined, as it does in externalising conversations, a range of possibilities becomes available to revise this relationship'.

You may hear or see this type of externalising conversation called a 'statement-of-position map'. This type of conversation includes four stages, which we will briefly outline below (as per White 2007), and illustrate with the help of Maeve and Sara.

Enquiry category 1: Negotiating an experience-near definition of the problem

Questions in this first stage are asked to help the person to name and define the problem as they see it and in their own words. We hope for a rich, detailed description of the problem and its characteristics. Some people might choose to use a metaphor here such as 'soggy cloud' to name and characterise low mood, or talk about the problem in terms of size, colour or shape. Where someone might struggle with this kind of description or want to stick with a label, we can help to externalise a problem by adding a 'the' – for example, 'the depression' – which helps to separate it from the person. When Sara invited Maeve to tell her more about how she understood her experience, Maeve let Sara know that she was interested in talking more about what she went on to name as 'The Anger'. Sara learned that The Anger tended to crop up in close relationships and especially alongside hurt and disappointment.

Enquiry category 2: Mapping the effects of the problem

At this stage, we invite the person to describe the effects the problem is having on their life. We might ask a question like, 'What does the soggy cloud get you doing?' or 'What does the worry get in the way of?' For Maeve, The Anger had her walking on eggshells, getting welled up inside, shouting and snapping, and in tears.

Enquiry category 3: Evaluating the effects of the problem's activities

At this point, we ask the person to evaluate what they think of the effects the problem is having on their lives. An example could be, 'What do you think about the way the worry gets you staying in the house and avoiding your friends?' People can sometimes be surprised at this question, but it is extremely helpful in the process of separating from the problem and moving to identify an alternative story, and can often help in bringing forward unexpected and meaningful perspectives. In Maeve's case, The Anger had her feeling a horrible, nasty person; hating it, hating herself and doing things she did not want to do. Maeve told Sara: 'The Anger is not me; it is taking me in the wrong direction'. Sara asked Maeve if she might have a sense of what the right direction would be, and she said that this would be in the direction of 'The Point Being Made'. Maeve came to notice that The Anger might be a prompt for her that something did not sit well. Sometimes this was due to a mismatch between Maeve's expectations of how things should play out as a result of making efforts and what actually took place, which would lead her to feel stupid for giving of herself and for trying, ready for The Anger to come in.

Enquiry category 4: Justifying the evaluation

Having identified how someone feels about the effects of a problem on their lives, we ask them why they feel that way. For example, 'Can you tell me why it isn't okay with you that you miss seeing your friends because the anxiety gets you staying in the house?' This enables us to hear about what is important to the person, providing a way into exploring values in life and a way into an alternative storyline, as we will see. Having identified that the direction she wanted to go in was The Point Being Made, Maeve was able to explain this for Sara and let her know that honesty, with herself and from others, was of paramount importance. Maeve explained that, in this respect, she had certain boundaries that should not be crossed – for example: 'I will not be used as a doormat; I will stand up for myself; I am a person with my own rights and thoughts and I am old enough to express them'.

Maeve's work with Sara provides a lovely example of where a conversation like this can then lead. Together, they went on to plot the history of The Point Being Made, its allies, what Maeve knew of its correspondence to her ideas about living life well and how she might bring The Point Being Made to its correct place. Maeve found that just being aware of The Point Being Made seemed to have her walking away from situations where The Anger had been running the show in the past. She noticed that she had been having more hugs with her husband, more chatting together and laughing, and fewer obstacles and rows.

Michael White (2007) describes this process of moving from describing and naming an action to a consideration of the meaning of this action as moving from the 'landscape of action' to the 'landscape of identity'. This process of moving back and forth through these domains in our conversations is something you may notice as you read other examples of narrative practice later in the book.

Re-authoring conversations

When we talk about a re-authoring conversation, we are referencing a particular way of plotting out different stories across the life course. This can feel particularly helpful in the context of working with older people, and with people living with dementia, who will often be more confident and able to share stories of their earlier life than to talk about the present.

As explained by Michael White (2007), this type of conversation has the objective of strengthening and thickening the more helpful alternative narratives that we are trying to draw out. It also mitigates against a particular story or event being dismissed or discounted as a 'one-off', as we look for other examples of how a particular initiative, idea or value has been present in someone's life over time. The telling of stories linked by a particular idea, action or intention can move back and forth through time and into the near future, when we may consider what the person may have learned about a step they may wish to take going forward. You can find examples of this in Chapter 5, when Viv traces different stories of being shown care in her life against a dominant story of neglect and abuse. Viv was able to find stories of care from her sister and from staff in a hospital setting, as well as observing care from friends' parents. This storyline moved forwards into Viv's adult life, where she experienced care from friends and neighbours and showed care to others, including her daughter and granddaughter, as she continued to do until her death.

We can often see the origins of a preferred way of being, such as 'keeping going', in very early life, which may connect the person with someone in their 'club of life' that they may not have thought about for a long time. In Chapter 4, Polly, Jane and Dan explain 're-membering conversations', which can provide a moving and beautiful way of reconnecting someone with people who have been important and influential in their life.

'Passing hope around' – collective narrative practice and therapeutic documents

It seems pertinent to conclude this chapter with a section about the emphasis on 'collective narrative practice', which we will focus on at different points during this book. David Denborough (2012, p.41) writes in detail about the history of collective narrative practice and describes it as an approach that 'seeks to respond to groups and communities who have experienced significant social suffering in contexts in which "therapy" may not be culturally resonant'. He describes many 'social' projects that have become central to aspects of narrative practice and outlines some of the initial work by David Epston, who began to collect the 'insider knowledge' of clients' 'wisdoms' into archives, so that these could be shared with people facing similar difficulties and challenges. Denborough (2008, p.51) writes too of the influential role of Cheryl White in the foundation of Dulwich Centre Publications, where the ethos was 'to open space and forums where a developing "culture" of non-pathologising practice could experience and manifest itself'. He also emphasises the role of narrative practice in terms of social action and challenging the taken-for-granted knowledges present within our culture. You will see many examples of collective practice of this type later in Chapters 8 and 9, when the authors share ways of using these ideas with groups of older people, people living with dementia and in work supporting colleagues.

This collective way of thinking about the people we work with also invites us to think how we might link people together in our individual therapeutic work, and the narrative therapy literature is rich with examples of this which have inspired us (for example, Denborough 2008; Whyte 2012). Sara and Maeve emailed women working in Sara's team with the subject line, 'Help please, ladies!' asking what they thought about how women should respond to The Anger and inviting them to share their stories. Later on in therapy, when Maeve had identified the importance of honesty and openness in her life, she and her grandchildren made a document called 'Grandma's Rules'. This enabled everyone to make their expectations and wishes clear, and to know that it was okay to be seen and heard when they were at Maeve's house. In Chapter 7, Helen shares how she linked people together using 'definitional ceremonies' and letter-writing. These letters and documents can be described as 'therapeutic documents', which form an important part of narrative practice, whether working with individuals or in groups. These can serve a number of functions, such as strengthening and thickening preferred stories, helping people hold on to important ideas or building hope and solidarity between people or groups. In Chapter 8, we see further examples of this in a group context, such as when Asesha worked with people with dementia and their care partners to create poems that were shared from one group to another.

As a group, we are drawn to the idea of 'passing hope around' (Whyte 2012). In the writing of this book, we hope that, in a similar vein, we are passing hope around with examples of narrative practice within our work with older people.

INVITATION TO REFLECT

- How do you feel embarking on this book?
- What are your hopes for exploring the use of narrative therapy with older people?

Recommended reading

Morgan, A. (2000) *What is Narrative Therapy? An Easy-to-Read Introduction.* Adelaide: Dulwich Centre Publications.

White, M. (2007) *Maps of Narrative Practice.* New York: W.W. Norton.

See the Dulwich Centre (https://dulwichcentre.com.au) and the Institute of Narrative Therapy (www.theint.co.uk) for introductory courses and a large range of reading materials and films.

CHAPTER 3

Discourses: The Stories That Shape Us

Sara Banks, Pete Ord, Polly Kaiser and Rosslyn Offord

A man is always a teller of stories, he lives surrounded by his own stories and those of other people, he sees everything that happens to him in terms of these stories, and he tries to live his life as if he were recounting it. (Sartre 2000, p.61)

What are discourses?

'When we meet with older people, the relationships we build are influenced by our previous experiences with older adults, by the messages we receive from society, and by the feelings we have about ageing ourselves' (Jeffery 2024, p.3). The stories or narratives of our lives, both in terms of the issues we face and our understanding of how we respond, are powerfully shaped by the wider stories within our communities and cultures.

'Discourse' is another word for these wider stories that are shaped and carried across generations, and which often serve the interests of a dominant group. Jeffery (2024) describes how we can understand discourses as 'frameworks of ideas' handed down to us by society. Sometimes we choose to adopt these as a way to understand ourselves and the world around us and find them helpful. However, much of the time these ideas are so much part of the wallpaper that we don't notice them, and they can become prescriptive without us even realising. Discourses can feel like 'truths', and we can fail to question how they have been arrived at or who decided that this is how the world should be.

Individuals and groups who sit outside what is regarded to be the dominant discourse can experience a sense of somehow failing to live up to socially decided 'norms', such as looking a certain way or achieving a particular standard or lifestyle.

Consider, for example, how much advice about parenting has changed over time – it would be unusual in Britain today to hear someone tell their child to 'be seen and not heard', yet this was still said routinely to children in the 1950s. Discourses about parenting also serve as an example of how these rules for living are shaped by factors such as culture, religion and class.

We can think about how different discourses shape the way we understand older people and people living with dementia too. The story of dementia has changed dramatically over time. The 'person-centred care movement' (Keady, Williams and Hughes-Roberts 2007) did not really become mainstream until the 1990s, yet it's hard to imagine now how radical the idea was that people living with a dementia could lead fulfilling lives (Kaiser 2017b), let alone be actively involved in research and committees, and speaking and writing about their experiences, which are all very common now in the UK.

Paying attention to discourses is fundamental to narrative practice, as it enables us to understand and work with the impact that social factors have on psychological distress. This chapter aims to introduce you to some of the discourses that impact on the way older people are seen and treated within our society and its institutions. Rarely do discourses operate independently, and the ways in which they interrelate or intersect will also be discussed.

It is important to note that it is beyond the scope of this chapter to cover all the possible discourses that might be associated with ageing, and the ones that are visible to us are, of course, specific to the time, country and cultures with which we are familiar as writers. There will be plenty of others, and we invite you to reflect on the ones that you notice in your life and particular context. We will begin with a consideration of ageism.

Discourses of ageing

Ageing discourses are dominated by 'ageism', a term that was coined by Robert Butler in the 1960s (Butler 1969). It can be defined as the discrimination against older people because of negative and inaccurate stereotypes. It is so ingrained in our culture that we often do not even notice. Indeed, ageism has been called one of the last socially accepted prejudices (Weir 2023). It is so embedded that it can be found in the form of 'institutional ageism': laws, rules, social norms, policies and practices that unfairly restrict opportunities and systematically disadvantage older people (World Health Organization [WHO] 2021). Often, seemingly neutral practices can have harmful repercussions, such as only providing therapy appointments online, which is arguably a form of 'digital ageism'.

Ageism can be internalised. It is not uncommon to hear older clients say things like, 'I don't want to bother the doctor,' thereby marginalising themselves in the process (Applewhite 2016; Macdonald 1984). Ageism has a huge impact and has been associated with earlier death by 7.5 years (WHO 2018).

The deficit discourse

The language we use is littered with ageist and deficit focused messages – for example, the idea that older people's thinking is rigid and no longer flexible ('you can't teach an old dog new tricks'). Perhaps this discourse explains why, in the UK, there has been such a historical discrepancy between mental health resources made available to older people compared to those for younger adults. Many clinicians do not refer older people for therapy as they believe it is somehow too late, and older people may refuse therapy for the same reason. Yet there is evidence that older people respond better to psychological therapy than younger adults (Saunders et al. 2021).

One common stereotype is that old age equals frailty and vulnerability. Deficit based discourses have also shaped our understanding of dementia, with a focus on individual decline and loss and on the neurocognitive aspects. These perceptions are not without consequences: we are led to form negative ideas and beliefs about identities of older people and to misinterpret their experiences. Take, for example, a common idea that it's 'normal' to be depressed or to become forgetful in old age, and what this might mean for trying to access support or treatment. In Chapter 8, you will hear how people with dementia describe stigma as the biggest challenge they face, and not memory or other impairments.

For those interested in reading more about these ideas we recommend Gergen (2009) and Madsen (2013).

Individualism

Another important discourse to consider is that of individualism. This is associated with the dominant neoliberal political system in western culture, in which the individual is seen as the source of meaning, identity and personal achievement (Davies 2021; White 2004a, p.131). We often hear from older people about the psychological challenges of retirement, the loss of identity or sense of uselessness experienced by those who have had to give up work or tasks by which they felt defined. This emphasis on individual achievement for identity and self-worth also prizes independence. We are regularly struck by how often older people, and people living with dementia, struggle with feeling a sense of shame or failure when they are unable to manage everything on their own. This can have the effect of feeling that they have less worth if they need assistance and fuels worries about 'being a burden'.

The healthy ageing discourse

As a possible counter-discourse to ageing as deficit and decline, the healthy ageing movement has been a strong influence in research, intervention and public policy (Stephens, Breheny and Mansvelt 2015). The healthy ageing discourse is also associated with what Rowe and Kahn (1997) describe as 'successful ageing' (Rubinstein and de Medeiros 2015), as well as 'productive ageing', but these are not without unintended negative consequences (Stephens and Breheny 2018). In Chapter 6, Karen and Rosslyn allude to this particular discourse, which led to Karen feeling that she was 'failing' at retirement by not persisting with travel and other activities that were not realistically available to her while caring for her husband. We can also see how this discourse is influenced by culture, class and, arguably, western neoliberal norms (Rubinstein and de Mederios 2015). Retirement is seen in very different ways by different groups.

Discourses of family

Across the world's cultures there is a diversity in terms of what 'family' means. However, as the idea of the nuclear family remains the dominant notion within western society (Eerola, Paananen and Repo 2023) this may serve to marginalise or even stigmatise families that do not conform. Think, for example, of the 'childless cat ladies' discourse, or the experience of older people without grandchildren, who may feel marginalised in social groups where grandchildren are a frequent source of conversation, comparison and status.

Intersectionality

These discourses, of course, do not impact in isolation on the lives and identities of older people. Life as it is lived is always more complex. 'Intersectionality' is suggested as a term to capture how different discourses may interact and to avoid a polarised understanding of older people's lives (Holman and Walker 2021). All older people are clearly not the same!

For example, older people might experience multiple layers of disadvantage due to their membership of several stigmatised groups. The phrase 'mutton dressed as lamb' communicates a more punishing set of standards for older women's appearance compared to those for older 'distinguished' looking men. We recognise the double jeopardy faced by older people of colour living in majority White countries, which lead to far poorer health outcomes (American Psychological Association 2020). We see the additional stigma and discrimination faced by people of colour who experience mental health difficulties and the additive effects of class and poverty (Joseph Rowntree Foundation 2017).

It would be impossible to even begin to imagine the experience of older people within the lesbian, gay, bisexual, transgender and queer plus (LGBTQ+) community without considering the intersecting effects of diverse discourses, their historical context (homosexuality is still illegal in many countries and was understood by the profession of psychiatry in Europe as a 'psychiatric disorder' until 1992) and what has happened to people as a result.

> **INVITATION TO REFLECT**
>
> - What are the discourses of ageing that you can think of in your context, and how might these relate to one another?
> - How far do you think they might affect the way you see yourself as you age or see older people around you?
> - What other effects do you think these discourses have on us all?
> - What might an awareness of these effects make possible in our lives?

Alternative discourses in relation to older people and dementia

Alternative discourses have been suggested, characterised by notions of personhood (Kitwood and Bredin 1992) and citizenship (O'Connor et al. 2022). These promote more positive possibilities, moving away from cognitive capacity and earning power as key sources of self-worth and instead putting the experience of the older person, or the person with dementia, at the forefront.

This recognition of the sense of agency of the person with dementia – that is, the ability to have and act on one's own preferences and make one's own choices – sees people with dementia as 'maintaining and asserting personhood, forming coalitions, claiming rights, becoming politically active, exercising agency, [and] taking control, risks and responsibilities' (Bartlett and O'Connor 2010, p.5). It also reflects the view that the loss of self commonly associated with dementia is determined by a failure in the social environment and quality of caring relationships rather than structural changes in the brain (Kitwood and Bredin 1992; Mitchell, Dupuis and Kontos 2013).

The literature is rich with examples of creative and community based projects and initiatives that support people to sustain their sense of identity, choice, citizenship and connections between different generations into later life. Many examples of this are shared in Chapter 8. These projects work within a different understanding of ageing, with a move away from difficulties and loss-focused discourses to discourses around creativity, connection, interdependency and fun. This allows for the bringing of new possibilities into people's lives, sense of identity and relationships, and for people to see themselves in a different, more helpful way. This was captured perfectly by one of the participants in a Tree of Life group when they said, 'I've found the new old me'.

As Sara illustrates in the examples that follow, narrative practices can provide a means of identifying the impact of various discourses within the wider context of people's lives, and to connect to preferred stories and ways of living that may lie outside of dominant discourses. You will see that some of these practices involve the use of externalising and re-authoring, introduced in Chapter 2 and re-membering, introduced in Chapter 4. Sara's work with Graham and Ron also illustrates a key theme in this book: that narrative practices take place in relation to the person's social, cultural, historical and political context. We invite you to consider how it might feel to have a conversation like the ones Sara describes.

Graham: Locating the problem in context and discourse and naming what this makes possible

Graham was referred to the clinical psychology service for support in managing thoughts and feelings associated with 'anxiety' and 'defectiveness'. I had been told that social interactions were difficult for Graham and that he had had a diagnosis of autism several years ago. As a result of retiring around 5 years earlier, Graham no longer felt fulfilled. He was involved in many activities that provided structure to his week and helped him to meet people. However, due to declining physical health, he was no longer able to undertake those activities that inspired him the most. Graham told me that he felt defective, and that this defectiveness was quite often present in social situations.

Our sessions began with me trying to understand a rich description of the problem(s) that Graham was having, and, if possible, to name this. As we saw with Maeve in Chapter 2, this process of externalising can help to dis-locate the problem, providing space for other possibilities to emerge. Graham spoke of The Controller, which had been around for as long as he could remember. Graham told me The Controller was smart, sensing his current situation or experience and then converting that into a positive or negative feeling. For example, if he was socialising or in an uncertain situation, it made him feel anxious; if someone told him he had done something well, it increased his self-esteem and made him feel accepted. When a negative feeling hit a particular threshold, The Controller would force him to back off or abandon something altogether. Following lots of consideration, Graham concluded that The Controller was much more disruptive than he had realised.

Together, Graham and I were able to explore the history of The Controller, and Graham recognised its inadequacy in being able to work out what might set off particular thoughts and feelings. This brought us to thinking about the role of social discourses in relation to the existence, actions and effects of The Controller.

The first discourse that Graham felt was relevant was in relation to rules around normality in social situations, where extraverts are admired and introverts are considered abnormal. He introduced me to several examples that counter this discourse: the *Room 5* programme on BBC Radio 4, where the author Holly Smale talks about being diagnosed as autistic in adulthood, and a document titled, 'The Eight Advantages' (Greenwood 2023). Graham sent me further reading: *Quiet: The Power of Introverts in a World That Can't Stop Talking* (Cain 2013). Graham had experienced first hand throughout his life the strength of the discourse that associates being quiet with being defective or antisocial, and he knew that he wasn't in agreement with this. In fact, contrary to this discourse, he was 'desperate for connection'.

Explicitly locating the problems in context led Graham to recognise that he had been trying to live life in line with the prescriptions, promises and 'small print' of some of these dominant discourses. In response he shared some of Holly Smale's words:

> It feels a bit like growing up thinking you're a duck and everyone telling you, your entire life, that you're a rubbish duck, and you try and do all the duck things…you try and swim, you try and catch worms and stuff like that…and you think I am the world's worst duck…and then…suddenly…someone says, 'You do realise you're not a duck, you're actually a frog?' And you have this moment of revelation…of course, it doesn't matter that I can't paddle and do all of those kind of duck things because I am really good at being a frog, I'm just not very good at pretending to be a duck. (Smale 2024)

Graham reflected that feeling fulfilled, inspired and alive was more important to him now than what The Controller and its underlying social discourses were dictating. Together, we identified the skills and abilities Graham had used in order to resist these forces. I heard stories about a range of initiatives Graham had taken: dancing; standing up for his beliefs and principles in relation to his own and others' health and safety; proactively denouncing the objectification of women; showing up for love in his parental duties; being complimented for his comic timing. He was reminded of his son saying he had a strong moral compass.

What came to emerge for Graham was a growing knowledge of 'What It Means To Be Me'. This is what Graham wants to say about this:

> Living life in line with my beliefs and principles is high up the pecking order for making big decisions, responding to and avoiding future regrets and in feeling better about myself. [This] has had a permanent effect on me. I can be more fluid with my actions, which will give rise to people interacting with me differently, so this is continually reinforced. I am going to practise doing what feels right in the moment; take opportunities that feel right in the moment; stand up for my beliefs and principles in the moment. It is making me feel I bring some value to the world – all things [that] were [previously] overshadowed by The Controller.

> Respect myself
>
> Categorisation of types of entities
>
> Demonstrate love and support for sons
>
> Feeling useful & valuable & *admired* & recognised & *respected*
>
> Proactively ensure problems get resolved
>
> Analysing and questioning information
>
> Demonstration of what it means to be me
>
> Being true to my authentic self and be assertive to enable this
>
> Reacting to opportunities
>
> Catch all phrases – How about you?
>
> Scientific process
>
> Parity of esteem
>
> *Standing up for my beliefs & principles (in zone)
>
> Focus on what's important & commitment
>
> Acts of courage
>
> Acts of determination & persistence
>
> Importance, and pursuit, of truth & integrity
>
> *Taking opportunities in the present moment to avoid regret

FIGURE 3.1 BEING ME (GRAHAM)

CONTEXT AND DISCOURSE MAP

The conversations summarised above used Holmgren, Hensing and Dahlin-Ivanoff's (2009) context and discourse 'map' as a guide. This drew out the wider social conditions and injustices affecting Graham's life and provided a scaffold for him to identify his knowledges and skills and the way in which these reflected his values, foregrounding a 'sub-story' of his life. The sense of agency Graham began to experience shines through in the way he found he could 'fluidly' stand up for his values moment by moment. This reflects the notion of 'the story lives us' rather than seeing narratives as a 'representation of life' (White 1995).

Ron: Working with 'failure conversations'

As you will see in other parts of the book, various 'maps' can help us to guide conversations in narrative therapy. These enable us to support people to move from familiar 'problem' stories and towards alternative stories that invite new possibilities for identity and for action.

White's 'failure conversations map' can be a helpful framework for conversations which acknowledge the effects of particular discourses. These discourses often lead people to conclude they have not adequately lived up to societal norms, expectations and standards and, in doing so, have somehow personally failed. This is an eight-stage enquiry which:

1. Identifies the ways in which someone may refuse to conform to social norms or expectations (the requirements of modern power).
2. Richly describes ways of thinking and living that do not fit with social norms and expectations.
3. Provides a way to recreate alternative, preferred identities.

See White (2004a) for a full description. With Ron's permission, I have used our session notes to illustrate the rich, uncharted territories and possibilities that the failure conversations map can lead us to with the people who come to see us.

A letter from the team psychiatrist told me that Ron had a long history of what they described as mental illness and a diagnosis of 'dysthymia', self-harm and alcohol dependence (for which he had over 20 years of abstinence through attending meetings of Alcoholics Anonymous – AA).

In my first meetings with Ron it was apparent that he knew himself and his problems very well indeed. He explained to me that he often felt threatened and imposed upon by the world. When this happened, he would, in his words, overreact, shout, withdraw, berate himself and then shut down. Together, we found a name for one of the problems he had experienced across the course of his life: The Self Preservation Barrier.

THE WALL

My heart's at bay behind a wall,
So small it's hardly there at all.
The wall gets higher every day,
Deadening each word I say.
What's left for those outside to see,
Is nothing like what's left of me.
I don't know how I came to be,
The dark emptiness defining me.
A stranger walks my steps and sleeps,
While my secret self in silence creeps,
In circles ever smaller still,
Bereft of purpose, lost, until,
Despairing any other choice,
I summon up a madman's voice,
And shout in bitter desperation,
A final plea for consolation.
But unheard echoes slowly die,
Like every secret tear I cry.
There is no answer I can see,
There's no escape for I am me.
I hurt and pain at least is real,
Nothing changes, there's no repeal.
My life is like a Cul-De-Sac,
No way forward and no way back.

BY RON W

Ron saw that The Self Preservation Barrier, which had once felt indispensable, now felt more like a prison or a burden. Although it enabled him to feel strong, confident and capable, this was at a cost and blocked his intuition. Ron told me that he wanted to experience things 'as me, not as my alter ego'. He also said that he wanted to be calm, kind and helpful.

Together, Ron and I considered the expectations, norms and

standards which he had been subjected to and had failed to live up to in life. The following paragraphs are Ron's words:

> Measuring up has been a large part of the tension I've experienced throughout my life. In recent times I have been unable to find a sense of normality or peace of mind to achieve any quality of life…Increasingly, my life has been one huge failure to cope…It produced an enormous sense of intolerability. I would wake and in moments experience a wash of dread and hopelessness that stayed with me throughout the day.
>
> I wouldn't want to be alive at that point. My life lessons taught me that I could cope with anything if I was strong enough, and if I couldn't find or do the right way then it would be a failure of mind that had me feeling inadequate – not brave, clever or strong enough. The putting down of myself is a large part of what makes it feel intolerable.
>
> I think that this yardstick comes from my early life which was one of a fairly regimented routine. With the foster children who lived with us, we were modelled and presented to the world as an ideal. We were told regularly by our parents that because we were in a stable family, we were luckier and needed to be stronger and right.
>
> We weren't given a great deal of detail as to what that actually represented and I read to escape: Lawrence of Arabia, Marvel Comics, Alexander the Great. I quickly realised that what I was reading described people in strong, heroic roles. I latched on to the idea that this was what the world applauds, that's what right looked like. That more things could be achieved through tenacity, strength, courage and superpowers.
>
> I knew I was failing at the inner strength aspect of this. I was lacking the capabilities to excel. Somehow, I had missed out on strength of character, courage, raw talent, intellect to excel, and I was therefore a failure.

Alongside the creation of The Self Preservation Barrier, Ron shared other ways in which he had made efforts to address these failures:

I wanted to be a doctor and for A levels I did the three sciences I was told I would need, despite not liking two of the three. Half-way through, I was told this wasn't necessary to go to medical school, and I was so angry. I had been misled. I did no more work and failed all three. As a result, I got into work – a reality check. I wasn't a doctor or a superhero. It felt pretty devastating.

I did the next best thing to reproduce what would be regarded as successful: I got myself a girlfriend, got married, a better job (even if I didn't enjoy it), got promoted, earnt lots of money, bought a house, got a company car and had foreign holidays. There was a shift at that time from socialist ideals to defining who we are through what we own. And I went for it! I taught myself information technology – I loved it and was good at it. My interests matched opportunities for pushing myself forwards.

Part of the role I was living at that time was as a husband and father. I was an authoritarian figure, insisting that my children should behave as ideal children. I was creating a perfect family my parents would admire. For many years it felt good.

I became a bartender at the local golf club. I had respect for the wealthy customers and would go along with whatever made them happy. I was accepted and rewarded in this role, and I got used to drinking. In my next job I worked for a brewery. With drink in me I was more relaxed, a little way off the feelings of intolerability, less threatened, inadequate, incapable. Those feelings just disappeared. Away from the drink, I didn't have a way of coping with life as it was.

Ron went further in noting occasions when he had stood against or refused these expectations, norms and standards:

I always went to church as a kid, and this is an example of an occasion when I have joined in with something by myself, for myself and did not feel uncomfortable in doing so. I sang in the choir for 3 years and went on to serve at the altar. I was active in the community of the church congregation. Having a spiritual outlook was important to me, and I never felt that I was playing a role in that respect.

In my teens I got too busy with life, and it wasn't until my rock bottom in my drinking that I returned to the church. I prayed that the drinking would be taken away from me or to have a stroke or a heart attack or die. Shortly after, I was presented with a situation where I was brought to a rehabilitation centre. I didn't know how to say no, and so I joined a group there and was honest with my workplace and let them know I needed time off. They had no idea.

Then there are the times I have been out and about in nature and seen and appreciated beauty, peace and the clearliness of the world around me. It feels good to be part of that without having to question any of these things.

One of my hobbies is photography, and I do this for pure enjoyment. Spending time taking photos, sorting, editing and learning from these has been enormously fulfilling. I have put these on Facebook and received very positive feedback. The recognition from others felt honest and genuine. This is something I am good at where The Self Preservation Barrier's opinion of my inabilities or inadequacies have not been upheld, but I do then experience doubt. I think, 'I have let the leash out for a bit, will it yank me back? How long will this be allowed to last before it's destroyed?'

The 12-step programme and work around that felt like a direct challenge to this. It emphasises self-knowing, self-acceptance and self-worth. The willingness for me to have asked for help then and now is an act that says, 'This is not who I am'. The Wombles [a community litter-picking group] is another thing where I am not playing a role. It's just a feeling that I can contribute to society when I am there. The Self Preservation Barrier would have said, 'You won't be comfortable. You won't be good at it,' but I have kept going. Twice I have taken my young granddaughter, and she is as proud as punch of Grandad.

Though my immediate family are aware of the impact of The Self Preservation Barrier, the freedom of my relationship with my grandchildren and rewards from that unconditional love are enormous. It never ceases to amaze me how much they accept me as I am. It gives me a lot of freedom. I can behave in funny ways without embarrassment. A lot of things I didn't do as a kid I can do now. I was at the park the other day and my granddaughter was charging ahead, and she shouted, 'Come on Grandad, skip!' so I did!

Ron and I reflected upon the further steps he had taken in building on efforts to live in line with what mattered. We tried to name what was most important and identify the foundations for Ron's values, principles, interests and efforts. He said:

If we don't do good things to feed this part of us, then the pilot light shrinks and fails. Meeting with AA friends, listening to them, sharing my experience produces a sense of fulfilment that is a direct challenge to The Self Preservation Barrier and role-playing. It's not bargaining – rather it's an instinctive feeling of inner strength, caring and well-being that comes. It is not transactional.

It's about openness, freedom, honesty, genuineness and fun. I went to the seaside with my wife and grandchildren the other day. I was able to see my ability just to sit and notice. I didn't have to change it or move on or run away. I could just contribute and be involved. I enjoyed the fun of it, being with them in the waves, being caught out for sneaking an ice cream, and didn't want it to end.

Religion is most powerful. I have always had an association with something greater than myself. All those ethical principles about love, selflessness, honesty. I also refer to fun as a guide. Just letting go and having fun. Also, the notion of knowing instinctively what right feels like, and that's not tied up in doing something or being remarkable, with heroics.

The books I read were always based around historic, heroic figures. But the notion of loyalty, responsibility and accountability are as relevant for me now as they were for The Self Preservation Barrier, which took these in a direction that was unhelpful. My father was a socialist, a union man. The ideas of living within communities without rules reinforce my ideas about honesty and rules and values that are socially acceptable.

Our conversations guided by the failure map closed with Ron expressing what it was like to live in a way that felt right. In Ron's words:

> It's a regenerative feeling of fun and joy. It's healing – it allows something to be repaired, and I am interested in this having more of a presence in my life. I want to promote honesty and openness, in contrast to my previous life, which was based on small dishonesties to protect myself and had my relationships with my family being incomplete.
>
> If I can do that, I'll have found a way forward that gives me hope. Before, I was retired, old and waiting to die. I couldn't see anything I wanted other than to just keep going. That has changed. I want more of what I am now experiencing. There are things we can do, places to go, hills to walk. I look forward to this now, doing more things together.
>
> I want 10 to 15 more years of enjoying the grandchildren, travelling, doing poetry and photography, being creative. I'm not done yet, for myself, my relationships and my future with The Self Preservation Barrier quite happily settled into a supporting, not a dominant, role. There's some acceptance and relief that it's no longer intervening. I'm more relaxed, I'm chatting to neighbours in a way I wasn't before, I am trusting myself and the newness. I react now as me as a whole. I wake up now and I want to get up. I have a fondness for my wife. We have plans together – things we can enjoy.

Ron's words show how the failure conversation map made it possible for him to reflect upon his life in relation to discourse, and the ways in which he was able to take steps towards living in line with his values and alternative rules for living.

Ron and I had met for several sessions before embarking on these failure conversations and have recently been in touch again. He reflected how these earlier meetings had helped him to identify The Self Preservation Barrier and get a different perspective on some of his deepest feelings; to recognise the origins and possible explanations for some of the things which were still hurting him.

Ron found the failure conversations had another effect. They seemed to thicken his preferred story, elucidate his sense of the next right move such that, in his words, 'They represented a series of advancements in understanding and acceptance, with each stage of the proceedings a necessary precursor to the next – a pattern which is recognisable in life as a whole'.

Closing comments

In this chapter, we have tried to introduce the effects of some dominant discourses around ageing, which have the power to shape how we see and treat each other individually, throughout society and within our institutions. We have provided some examples of how some of these discourses show up in conversations we have with older people who have accessed mental health services and, through this, offered some suggestions around how narrative practices might support us to approach these hidden and often tricky issues, and where this might take the people we work with and, of course, ourselves – personally and professionally.

A lasting and ongoing effect of consciously exploring social discourses with the people who come for therapy is that while this work may have the effect of shrinking the size of an often long-standing sense of shame and inadequacy, it also brings challenges. Specifically, raising our own and others' awareness of the wider injustices that affect our lives also brings to the fore the knowledge that we cannot be alone. There is a risk that, without an immediate and active network to tackle these injustices, we might all feel frustration and powerlessness to address these. Some of the learning here is that the ideal outcome when using a narrative approach is not at the individual level, but in the creation of possibilities for social change to tackle injustices. As the needs of older people are widely under-represented and under-resourced, this cannot come to fruition without a call to action to begin to address this gap.

It feels appropriate to finish with a reconceptualisation of ageing, moving from seeing ageing as decline to ageing as a dynamic process involving constant and continuous change. A sense of being valued and making a meaningful contribution to society are important in maintaining good mental health in old age. A sense of place, belonging and good neighbourhood relationships with positive physical environments and spaces are vital. Put in other words, 'When we're younger, we need a boost as we get moving, but as we age, we gather momentum through the build-up of experiences and insights' (Sweetland, Volmert and O'Neil 2017, p. 26).

Recommended reading

Gergen, K.J. (1973) 'Social psychology as history'. *Journal of Personality and Social Psychology 26*, 309–320.

Gergen, K.J. (2009) *Realities and Relationships: Soundings in Social Construction*. Cambridge, MA: Harvard University Press.

Holmgren, K., Fjällström-Lundgren, M. and Hensing, G. (2013) 'Early identification of work-related stress predicted sickness absence in employed women with musculoskeletal or mental disorders: A prospective, longitudinal study in a general population'. *Disability and Rehabilitation 35*, 5, 418–426.

Jeffery, S. (2024) *Deconstructing Ageing: A Workbook for Continuing Professional Development and Reflexivity*. Manchester: Greater Manchester Mental Health NHS Foundation Trust.

Madsen, W.C. (2013) *Collaborative Therapy with Multi-Stressed Families*. New York: Guilford Press.

White, M. (2004) *Narrative Practice and Exotic Lives: Resurrecting Diversity in Everyday Life*. Adelaide: Dulwich Centre Publications.

CHAPTER 4

'Like the Voice of a Bird Singing in the Rain, Let Grateful Memory Survive in the Hour of Darkness'

USING NARRATIVE PRACTICES TO SCAFFOLD HELPFUL CONVERSATIONS ABOUT LOSS AND DYING

Polly Kaiser, Daniel Blake and Jane Grant

Give sorrow words; the grief that does not speak whispers the o'er-fraught heart and bids it break.
—SHAKESPEARE, *MACBETH*

Neither the sun nor death can be looked at steadily.
—FRANCOIS DE LA ROCHEFOUCAULD,
REFLECTIONS; OR SENTENCES AND MORAL MAXIMS

Introduction
Polly
Not long after qualifying I was asked to see June, an active 74-year-old woman. The referral was for 'anxiety'. It transpired that the trigger for the anxiety was the anniversary of her son's death. He had died, tragically, aged 8 years old, many years before. I knew the therapy wisdom of the time said I was supposed to help her come to terms with his

death and help her say a final goodbye. I couldn't do that, and neither could she.

To introduce ourselves, the three authors of this chapter cover the life span of careers from early, mid to semi-retired. As well as stories from our clients, like June, we also want to share stories of loss and hope from personal and professional perspectives and the narrative practices we have found most helpful.

This will involve sharing conversations we have had in the therapy room, in groups and conversations we have had with colleagues and teams. Personally, this work can be challenging as it can bring to mind our own losses, our feared losses and fears about our own mortality. All authors speak and write from having had their own personal losses. One of our major challenges, as therapists and community workers, may indeed be a fear of 'going there'. We offer this chapter in the hope that the ideas we explore help you as much as they have helped us.

Cultural context

How we talk about death, dying and loss has an influence on how we approach it in our culture, society and with our own family and friends. Ways of responding to loss, death and dying are socially constructed and practices change throughout time and cultures (Aries 1982; Gergen 1985). Years ago, a 'good death' meant that anyone could come into the space around the person; neighbours and strangers received communion as a dying person was given the last rites; 'What is now deemed a private affair was once very public' (Kaiser 2017a, p.190).

Elisabeth Kübler-Ross's pioneering work *On Death and Dying* (1969) has been hugely influential on our cultural and therapeutic discourses for many decades. During the relief work she did across Europe, in the aftermath of the Second World War, Kübler-Ross observed how people coped with unimaginable losses and death. Given the 'keep calm and carry on' aspect of culture at that time, which was a necessary way of surviving, it is perhaps no wonder that the dominant social discourse was to 'move on'. That is what thousands of people across Europe were doing, literally and metaphorically. This, along with her subsequent psychiatric training in the United States, led her to her theory and ideas about the stages of grief, which has formed a dominant story about how we 'should' cope with death and dying, namely: denial, anger, bargaining, depression and acceptance (Kübler-Ross 1969). Others built on and modified her theory, like Colin Murray-Parkes (1972), who also talked about 'moving on', and later Worden (1983) with his 'tasks of mourning' where one is expected to 'say a final farewell'.

These ideas can be helpful; however, it is also important to notice the harm that can be caused if theories such as this are taken as objective truth rather than ideas or metaphorical guides for conversations (Gergen 1985; White 1988).

> I find the whole stages of grief thing quite interesting, because nobody talks about stages of falling in love, for example, or things like that, and I think it is a way of people distancing themselves, taming the experience, which is actually an experience that can't be tamed. It's one of these things that strips the flesh off your bones, and that is the truth about it. There aren't any neat stages, and there is nothing that can be identified as recovery, either, although obviously you learn to live with it, and through it, and differently because of it. But certainly, as soon as people talk about recovery, I just think, 'Ah, it hasn't happened to you yet'. (Pat Barker quoted in Clark 2015)

We can see that these meanings and practices, such as 'saying goodbye', can become 'taken-for-granted' realities about how one 'should' grieve. These ideas are, however, socially constructed and can and do change over time. Interestingly, Kübler-Ross herself, in later life, noted that the stages are not a linear and predictable progression and that she regretted writing them in a way that was misunderstood (Kübler-Ross and Kessler 2005). Poignantly, as she approached her own death, she acknowledged that you never get over the loss of a loved one but rather you learn to rebuild yourself around the loss you have suffered (Kübler-Ross and Kessler 2005).

Narrative practices have been part of this culture change. Rather than using the 'saying goodbye' metaphor, Michael White posed a different question. What would it be like if we used the 'saying hullo' metaphor (White 1988)? He does not overly critique traditional ideas, but points out that they can, and often do, induce a sense of failure for people, clients and therapists alike. As you will read, people report beating themselves up for 'failing to grieve properly' or 'move on'.

White (1997) shared his ideas that people's identities are shaped by what can be referred to as a 'club of life' and that it might be helpful for people to recall these, especially to support preferred identities through re-membering conversations. These ideas and, importantly, practices developed by White and others, such as Lorraine Hedtke (Hedtke 2003; Hedtke and Winslade 2004), came as a breath of fresh air into the therapy room. Hedtke worked in a palliative care context and usefully built on White's work.

Club of life and re-membering practices

Influenced by the work of anthropologist Barbara Myerhoff (see the box below), White (1997) developed the idea that people's identities are shaped by what can be referred to as a 'club of life', made up of members who have had particular parts to play in how we have come to experience ourselves (Russell and Carey 2002, 2004). He introduced Myerhoff's term 're-membering' into narrative therapy to describe helping people bring to the fore those from their life who support their preferred identity and preferred actions. Those in someone's club of life do not have to be directly known to be identified as significant to people's lives. For example, they may be the authors of books or characters in movies or comics, the stuffed toys of a person's childhood or a favourite pet (Russell and Carey 2002, 2004). Thinking about one's club of life offers new possibilities for therapeutic conversations that allow for direct acknowledgement of the contribution of others in their lives (White 1997).

Even if we are working with people with no family left, we can work with their club of life and reconnect them to these vital re-memberings. As Barbara Wingard so eloquently puts it, 'When we see ourselves through the loving eyes of those who have cared for us our lives are easier to live' (Wingard and Lester 2001, p.43).

White (1988) wrote of resisting conversations focused on saying goodbye and instead focused on opening up the possibility of reclaiming a lost relationship:

Those questions that seemed most helpful in assisting persons to reclaim these important relationships were the ones that invited a recounting of what they perceived to be the deceased person's positive experience of them.... These questions had an immediate and visible effect. (White 1988, p.32)

RE-MEMBERING PRACTICES

Michael White (1988, 1997) was heavily influenced by Barbara Myerhoff, an anthropologist who worked with older Jewish people in southern California who had suffered great losses due to the Holocaust. She noted how they continued to honour and remember: maintaining memories in the present. She writes:

> To signify this special type of recollection, the term 're-membering' may be used, calling attention to the reaggregation of members, the figures who belong to one's life story, one's prior selves, as well as significant others who are part of the story. Re-membering, then, is a purposive, significant unification, quite different from the passive, continuous fragmentary flickerings of images and feelings that accompany other activities in the normal flow of consciousness. (Myerhoff 1982, p.111)

White (2007, p.140) proposed a re-membering conversations map to assist people to reengage with significant figures in their club of life along with the history of these important relationships. He proposed the following areas for consideration:

- *The figure's contribution to the person's life:*
  e.g. What strengths and attributes did Jack have? What was it you enjoyed about Jack?
- *The person's identity through the eyes of the figure:*
  e.g. If you could see yourself through Jack's eyes right now, what would you be noticing about yourself that you could appreciate?

> - *The contribution the person made to the life of the figure:*
>   e.g. What did Jack love and find valuable about you? What do you think you might have brought to Jack's life?
> - *The implications of this contribution for the figure's identity:*
>   e.g. What do you think the relationship Jack had with you helped him to know about himself? What do you think Jack would say if he could hear this conversation?

In addition to the club of life and re-membering practices, there are several other ideas from narrative practice that we, our clients and our colleagues have found particularly helpful which we will be illustrating in our stories. These are witnessing practices, including outsider witness and witnessing positions (see Chapter 7 for a fuller explanation of this); deconstructing conversations, including double listening; re-authoring conversations bringing forth stories of skills and competence; and solidarity teams and therapeutic documents. We give examples of all of these in this chapter, but for those who would find it helpful to know more about these, please refer to Chapter 2.

These practices, and especially re-membering practices, have been something all the authors have found invaluable in our work. We hope that the stories we are about to share illustrate how these new knowledges can support people to make new choices that help them to 'move on' in their lives, without necessarily forfeiting their relationship with the person they have lost. In having these conversations, we hope to assist the person to 'incorporate the lost relationship', which White (1988) points out can be particularly powerful.

Stories of responding to loss using re-membering practices

Let's now return to June. What helped her was talking about her son. She had been so afraid to open her box of grief that she had lost all connection with him which grieved her even more. Asking re-membering questions helped June to reclaim her son so that the pain of his loss was slightly more bearable. This process eventually led to her being able to put his photo on her mantelpiece and talk about him with her surviving children, something she had never been able to do before. They, too, could reclaim their brother.

Jane

I saw Arthur, a man in his 70s and experiencing low mood. He described himself as 'the black sheep of the family'; it felt to me like his story was very dominated by problems. I tried to listen out for times when the problems were not so powerful. I asked more questions for us to think about these times together. As we did, I could hear a new story emerging of him being someone who had managed to somehow keep him and his sisters together as a family unit following the untimely death of their parents when they were teenagers.

Some 60 years later they remained close and in one another's lives. In talking about this Arthur realised that he no longer did much of the 'keeping the family together', as this role had passed on to his nieces. At this point, I invited him to have a re-membering conversation with his parents about what they would think about him keeping the family together under such difficult circumstances and now having passed this on to the next generation. I think the second part of re-membering conversations, incorporating the lost relationship, was what was most helpful. By asking questions such as, 'If you could see yourself through your parents' eyes right now, what would you be noticing about yourself that you could appreciate?' I could see an immediate and visible effect which was very moving for both of us. He became emotional and said he thought they would be proud of his determination, strength, and protective and caring nature. That it would mean a lot to them that they were all in each other's lives, continuing to love and support each other.

This is an example of how narrative questions can bring about a new, enriched acknowledgement and validation of the self, an enriching of preferred identity. We then richly described all the skills 'keeping us together' had involved. I built on this, as it provided a platform for preferred ways of living, by asking: 'What difference will knowing what you know about yourself make to your next steps?; this helped translate this new knowledge into action for himself. This is an example of how re-membering and re-authoring practices can be used to help move someone from what is 'known and familiar' ('I am different, a failure') to what is 'possible to know' ('I've kept my family together for decades through the most difficult of circumstances and inspired others to carry this on for the next generation'). (See Chapter 2 for further information about these concepts.) Had I simply said this, it would not have had the same impact that the re-membering conversation had. The questions helped him discover it for himself in a way we could both feel in the room.

Old age can bring with it many losses, not just of people but loss of role, physical capabilities and ways of coping. These can have a huge impact on a person's preferred identity. Often, the conversations we are invited to have focus on adjustment and loss. This reminds me of conversations I had with Anne, who was living with the effects of macular degeneration and a stroke. Her husband told me that she was getting upset in the morning watching people go off to work. She expressed a great sadness at not being able to continue to work. I listened to her feelings about this and drew on double listening and the absent but implicit, as explained in Chapter 2, to consider what this distress was communicating about what was important to her but might be missing in her life. I heard that this was about contributing, working hard and being the head of the family. When she became aware that she had forgotten and became confused, it made her feel like she could no longer be respected as the head of the house. She talked about her two grandchildren who were only teenagers, but both had jobs, had a plan of what they wanted their career to be and were working hard to make this happen. She expressed immense pride that they had such a strong, dedicated work ethic. I enquired where they might have learned this from, and she thought perhaps it was something that she had instilled in her family as something to be valued. She pointed to a ring that her granddaughter had bought her with her first wage.

At this point, the words of my supervisor Hugh Fox came into my mind; he often talked about a metaphor of 'splicing', which is where the two parts of a rope that is broken are joined together by weaving the strands through each other. He referred to this when people have been through some sort of loss that means they have become disconnected from who they are and their values. He likened the work we do as trying to splice together the values a person previously held dear with the new version of themselves that is now living with a loss. In the process, it becomes clear to the person that they have not been separated from these precious values, but that they continue to express them in their life after the loss, and thus a sense of continuity is achieved where before there had been a sense of discontinuity.

These ideas led me to wonder how I might help Anne to stay connected to her values of contributing, working hard and being respected, despite what she had lost of her physical health. We used her ring as a tactile way of her holding close so that, even though she could not go out to work, she had contributed to the work ethic of her grandchildren. She could sit back as her work was being continued by others. I invited her to share stories of the history of these values, using the idea of re-authoring, discussed in Chapter 2. This helped Anne re-author her story from one of feeling a failure to one of still contributing the values of hard work being handed down, which she had in tangible form in the ring. Anne's family were able to prompt her to feel the ring, which helped to connect her to these important values with a sense of pride which helped her to cope with her feelings of sadness and loss.

It is not just individuals who feel losses. This can happen in our work teams too. While changes are a constant in life and in the NHS, there are life cycles to teams and losses that can be deeply felt. There are also losses 'held' by teams, such as the one Dan facilitated during Covid-19.

Stories responding to loss – working with groups and teams
Dan

I used narrative ideas to guide me when I was asked to meet with staff teams who had been caring for people with terminal illness during the Covid-19 pandemic. My invitation was to meet with three connected teams spanning the community and hospital contexts that worked with people who were dying and their families. Covid-19 had brought additional stress and barriers for the staff teams, a huge increase in hospital admissions, families not being able to be with their loved ones and an incredible amount of strain on the services. The management were concerned about staff well-being, and there was a growing discourse across the NHS about staff 'burnout'.

Reynolds (2011b) has taught me to be critical of the individualistic discourses that locate burnout within the individual, as a symptom of them not being 'resilient enough' to do the work. Staff told heartbreaking stories of the death and dying they had witnessed and the toll this had taken on them and the families of those who had died. In listening I was not searching for how they needed to cope but rather I noticed how these teams of people were able to come together and support each other, such as the stories they told of 'shouldering' each other up and the care and compassion they showed to their patients and their families. I was curious about the values that drew them to and sustained them in this work. As the teams were large, I was also aware of my limitations in not being able to reach all the staff members during each monthly session, which led to a use of therapeutic documents to help the wider teams witness 'sparkling moments' (Fox 2003).

These are moments when the client, or in this case the team, may feel more positive. They can also be described as the cracks where the light gets in (Cohen 1992). Our job is to identify instances when 'the problem' did not completely dominate. I asked about and noticed sparkling moments such as staff sitting with patients and offering them companionship while they waited for a scan, or sitting with family members at home and listening to them express how they were feeling in relation to their loved one being ill. A particularly moving example of a sparkling moment was where a staff member accompanied a patient who got married in the hospital grounds before she sadly died.

While respecting confidentiality, I wrote a summary letter after each session which was sent to all members of the invited teams. I drew out themes from our talking and posed questions to scaffold further talking and reflection around values and alternative storylines. Feedback highlighted that the letters helped everyone to feel involved, even when they could not attend. Not only did this consolidate what had been talked about; it also supported their values of solidarity and shouldering and further reflection outside of the sessions.

I used narrative ideas of 'witnessing positions' from Weingarten (2000, 2003, 2010) to consider how I could be with the teams as a witness (see the box below). I asked myself how I could remain aware and empowered as a compassionate witness. I acted into this position by re-membering with the team their relationships with patients who had died. I asked them what the patient had said to them during their time together, what feedback they had received from the patient's family and to re-member conversations with colleagues. I heard powerful narratives of how the staff had worked closely with the individual and their family to give them the death that they wanted and that was in line with their preferences. I started to hear clues to strong values around advocacy as a team that we could explore further and the teams could draw on moving forwards.

WITNESSING POSITIONS

Weingarten (2000) outlines how a witness is created anytime there is a victim and perpetrator. In this context, the 'perpetrator' was Covid-19 and the victims were those who were dying. People can change positions or be in multiple positions. I was aware that the staff teams were witnessing the effects of Covid-19 on their patients, and I was also a witness to their struggles as professionals and how Covid-19 had affected their lives, and indeed all our lives. Weingarten highlights four positions we can occupy as a witness that vary relating to how aware we are of being a witness and how empowered we are to act or do something about what we see. The sought-after position is the one in which we are aware of what we are witnessing and feel empowered to respond, acknowledge and act on what we have witnessed.

It felt important to me to find ways of supporting the team that did not risk suggesting that individuals should be more resilient but kept the focus on 'justice doing' (Reynolds 2019). There were a few ideas that helped me with this, including asking the attendees who is on their 'solidarity team' (Reynolds 2011b, 2012). These lines of enquiry helped to expand or 'thicken' a sense of the collective and being in this together. The attendees explored how they support each other at work and who, from their personal and professional relationships, shared their ethics, 'shouldered' them up and 'stood alongside' them.

Asking the team about their skills, values and what they hold most dear in their practice helped them to reclaim their expertise around supporting people at the end of life. These local knowledges were in turn used to influence and collaborate on wider organisational practices around death and dying – for example, the introduction of family areas on the wards. In Chapter 9, we discuss further ways narrative practices can be used to support ourselves and our colleagues.

Supervision
Jane

As we mentioned at the beginning of this chapter, grief work can feel challenging. Listening for 'sparkling moments' in the face of horrendous loss and tragedy can be difficult. So, one vital way we support each other to 'go there' is through supervision.

I had such a supervision conversation with my colleague, who wanted time to think about her work with Mike, in order to support him as best she could. Mike's wife was living in a care home and their conversations focused on Mike's feelings of grief and loss. Mike was feeling bullied by the dominant discourses about how people 'should' grieve and 'move on', as others commented on what he was doing and judged him for 'putting her away'. Not unusually, everyone in the family was grieving in separate ways. As my colleague spoke about their work, I heard her talking about what I thought was a sparkling moment, when she said to Mike that it sounded like he was showing his grandchildren a different way to grieve and get through such a difficult experience in life. My colleague had the sense that this moment meant a great deal to Mike, as it did to her.

In using narrative ideas about values and the restorative aspect of supervision, I really wanted to spend time finding out why this moment meant so much to her. I heard about how what was important to her was guiding her in the type of conversations she was having with Mike. This allowed my colleague to resist dominant discourses about what Mike was 'lacking', or what coping skills he needed, and focus on Mike's preferred identity. My colleague said, 'It felt like we were just two people in a room dealing with the toughness of life; we were equals'. Together we reflected on how our supervision discussions sustain us within our work. When talking about how she has found being introduced to narrative ideas, such as re-authoring, moving from a story of failure to a story of competence, she reflected, 'It's so helpful, it's like I know the approach I am taking with Mike is legitimate, an okay way to go'.

I took this to my own supervision with Dan and he reflected, 'I was struck by how Jane had noticed and attended to this sparkling moment and how skilfully she had thickened the significant stories of competence for both her colleague and for Mike. I was reminded of the ideas of supervision as re-authoring conversation (White 1997) and wanted also to linger here in this moment for Jane and consider the significance of this conversation for her'. I have reflected on the value of supervision for us as practitioners in helping us to deconstruct deficit discourses and connect instead with values and stories of competence that enable us to find ways to 'go on' together in this work (Shotter 2009).

Spirituality
Polly

For many, particularly at times of emotional stress, such as illness or bereavement, spirituality can be very important (Royal College of Psychiatrists 2009). It is not uncommon for people to think in spiritual terms and even if they do not, people around them do with condolences such as 'They've gone to a better place.' Spiritual conversations can be of vital importance and might be an untapped asset or strength for a person (Koenig, McCullough and Larson 2001; Levin 2001).

It may be that conversations around spirituality are part of your therapy. For some people, depending on their generation and cultural background, venturing into this territory can seem fraught with potential difficulty and it may just feel safer 'not to go there'. Although understandable, this may not be helpful, as such conversations have the potential to help us understand people and help them to feel safe and recognise the strengths they have. We hope that you will be able to connect with some of the ideas here to open up other avenues of conversation.

'Spirituality' may mean different things to those who believe in God and those who don't. Either way, we are often compelled to ask ourselves about the meaning and purpose of life. Spirituality is a more all-embracing concept than religion.

Goldsmith's (2004) definition of spirituality seems relevant and helpful as it links powerfully to the values of narrative practice: 'a commitment to honour a person's identity, to find meaning for his or her life, to encourage the possibility of relationship and to sustain a compassionate and secure environment in which the person can feel safe'.

> **SUGGESTIONS FOR QUESTIONS TO SUPPORT CONVERSATIONS ABOUT SPIRITUALITY**
>
> Ask if people would like to talk about such matters and then use the language they use, as words such as 'spirituality' and 'faith' can mean different things to different people.
>
> - Would you be interested in talking about how your faith/religion/spirituality have been impacted by your loss?
> - What role does faith/religion/spirituality play in your life or in coping with hard times?
> - If a person is part of a faith community, what role does it play in their life and in hard times?
> - How do you connect with God, spirituality, your religion or faith community?
> - How do the values we have been talking about link to your faith/spirituality/religion?

Conclusion

Therapy can be challenging. However, we are unlikely to go through our lives and careers without experiencing losses, professionally or personally. Our hope is that we have given you enough of a flavour of our experiences with narrative practices to illustrate how they offer different ways of supporting people that we, our clients and colleagues have found particularly helpful in this area of loss.

For those reading as therapists, we hope that some of what we have written may help sustain you in your values, 'going on', standing 'shoulder to shoulder' and 'justice doing', not just for your clients and your teams but also, vitally, for yourselves. We can all be challenged and changed by the work we do and our professional and personal experiences of loss.

We hope that we have shown that narrative practices help, and end with a poem from Polly.

Grief Legs
I've got my grief legs on today.
Heavy...
Ten Tun Boot Legs
Barely put one foot in front of the other legs
Heavy...
How can I move?
If I move from the place of grief
does it mean I have moved further away from you?
I want to stay in a cocoon of grief that keeps you close to me.
But I cannot stay
In this curled up
crawled up
Gnarled up
Place.
I need to stretch my toes
step out of bed
And slowly
Put one foot
in front of the other.
I do not want to go further away
I go forwards
Towards a life
without you physically in it
Towards the mundane
'Give us this day our daily bread'
life.

I've got my grief legs on today.
But I must step out,
step out to
feel the cool air on my cheeks,
The sun on my face
To see the sunshine on the river
Sparkling.
To smell the earth
The earth beneath my feet
where you will soon be resting
Resting...
While I put one foot
in front of the other
As I grieve for my mother.

(POLLY KAISER COPYRIGHT 02.03.2021)

INVITATION TO REFLECT

- Are any of the ideas in this chapter new to you?
- What has struck you, if anything?
- What is similar or different?
- Does supervision sustain your values? If so, how?
- Who is in your personal or professional 'club of life', and who has influenced you in terms of your thinking in this area so far?
- How might you hold them in mind during this work?

Useful resources

Use of outsider witnesses to facilitate conversations about end-of-life care with people with a diagnosis of dementia and carers – Dementia Engagement & Empowerment Project (DEEP) and Together In Dementia Everyday (TIDE): www.youtube.com/watch?v=3hqR8DzS4b8&t=13s

Dementia Voices (2018) *End of Life Care* and Post Bereavement Support – *Shifting the Conversation from Difficult to Important*. www.innovationsindementia.org.uk/wp-content/uploads/2018/09/End-of-Life-Care-Post-Bereavement-Support-Shifting-the-Conversation-from-Difficult-to-Important41.pdf

Pennine Care NHS Foundation Trust:
www.penninecare.nhs.uk/infoforcarers

CHAPTER 5

Using Narrative Therapy with Older People Who Have Experienced Trauma

STRENGTHENING STORIES OF RESISTANCE AND
GIVING VOICE TO WHAT IS PRECIOUS

Rosslyn Offord, Jane Grant and Polly Kaiser
with contributions from Vivienne Lowe and Becky Scullion

Mary was a caring and creative woman with a great deal of empathy for people – everyone, that is, except herself. She had grown up with a 'depressed mother' who would go to bed for days at a time – not only absent from Mary's life but leaving her wondering, 'What have I done wrong?' She married a man who, by all accounts, had been equally emotionally absent from her. When her much wanted daughter was born, she had an extremely traumatic birth in which they both nearly died. She was unable to have more children. She experienced post-natal depressed mood, flashbacks from the birth and nightmares. Her struggles to elicit help resulted in her being admitted to a psychiatric ward where she received electroconvulsive therapy. These experiences compounded her earlier birth trauma and silenced her expression of distress, which she lived with for many years. When she became ill in older age and needed hospitalisation, her earlier trauma and fears were reignited.

Narrative ideas about trauma

In this chapter, we shall share our experiences of using narrative practices to assist people, like Mary, whose ability to live their lives in the way they want has been affected by their experience of trauma.

Older people who speak with us will rarely use the language of 'trauma'. For us, it feels important to discuss this issue, as we have witnessed how ageist ideas have got in the way of them being able to find assistance with memories that cause distress. One idea is that it is 'too late' to do anything about it. Another is that, despite evidence to the contrary (Chaplin et al. 2015; Saunders et al. 2021), older people can't use psychological therapy or don't want to. We have even encountered the idea that early life trauma is not relevant to older people. On the contrary, we have found this subject to be of major relevance and interest to older people. Using narrative ideas, we have found ways of working that we have found to be immensely helpful. Viv, whose story follows later in the chapter, has expressed her desire to offer hope to others. This is why this chapter is here.

Before we continue, it is important to clarify what we mean when we talk about trauma. A psychological definition of trauma is very particularly defined as an 'individuals' response to an event or series of events that completely overwhelms their ability to cope and to integrate it into their life's narrative' (Stroniska, Szymanski and Cecchetto 2014, pp.13–18). When we use this word, we are therefore referring to a broad range of experiences. This could be a catastrophic event, such as an accident or experience of war, or a series of events, such as abuse or severe neglect.

Over the past decade or so, there has been an increased understanding of the longer term impact of difficult experiences in childhood, which have come to be known as ACEs or adverse childhood experiences (Felitti et al. 1998). For those people who have experienced a greater number of ACEs, there is an increased vulnerability to a range of both physical and mental health conditions. We frequently come to learn that these ACEs are present in the lives of the older people who consult us, even if they initially seem to come to us about something completely different.

In writing this chapter, we want to acknowledge that the concept of trauma itself can have different meanings for different groups of people and across generations. We recognise that the concept of trauma arguably carries its own set of discourses, and we share concerns about the ways in which an industry appears to have developed around trauma (Kiyimba et al. 2022). Following Vermeire (2023), we have tried to stay close to the language used by those we work with, who inform us about how best to understand the experiences they have lived through.

Old age and re-emerging trauma

In the contexts in which we work, it is not unusual for people to share early experiences of trauma which have been buried for many years; the person may have gone on to live their life without reference to what happened in the past, and on many occasions has never told anyone about these experiences. However, as people age, these earlier experiences can be triggered. Mikhailova (2015) described this as a 'domino effect', whereby later life challenges seem to reignite past traumas. There may be many reasons for this, which are often associated with the physical, social and cognitive changes that occur with ageing. For example, cognitive change may mean that a person may become less able to bury or suppress a difficult memory. Changes in physical health, such as pain due to osteoarthritis or cognitive change, might evoke feelings of vulnerability or fear. Even if not voiced, 'the body keeps the score' (van der Kolk 2015). Feeling vulnerable or fearful might bring back associations with early memories. Experiences of loss, such as bereavements or loss of job roles, like the ones we shared in the previous chapter, may also bring up feelings of vulnerability.

Narrative theory and practice and trauma

There are some theoretical ideas about working with trauma from a narrative perspective that underpin the work we want to share (see box below). An important idea is that trauma gets in the way of someone's 'sense of themselves' (White 2006). We therefore seek to help people to reconnect with what it is that they value and gives them meaning in their life. We can do this by careful 'double listening', listening out for the untold story (Kaiser and Blake 2022), and the 'absent yet implicit'

(Carey, Walthers and Russell 2009), as explained in Chapter 2. We listen to how people have responded to the trauma they experienced and explore what this might tell us about what they value and hold precious. Various authors (Lin Lee 2013; White 2006; Yuen 2009) have shared helpful ways of asking about responses to trauma which help to create a sense of agency, as well as hope, and to stand in a different position in relation to trauma.

> **NARRATIVE IDEAS ABOUT RESPONDING TO TRAUMA, FROM WHITE (2006)**
>
> 1. Everyone responds to trauma. This response may be to hide or stay silent or to not respond, or it may be to do something, such as run or fight, challenge or provide comfort.
> 2. Behind this response is an intention.
> 3. This intention will be connected with a belief or value.
> 4. By working with the belief or value, we can assist the person to connect with what it is they hold precious in their lives. This can then provide a foundation to build and strengthen this preferred identity or set of identities.
>
> In other words, we work with the person's response to the traumatic event rather than the event itself.

In our work with older people who have experienced trauma, we therefore have in mind working with their responses to trauma rather than the trauma itself. In listening out for what this may tell us about what the person gives value to, we explore who else may have been important in learning about what is precious or in helping someone know how to act.

As we try to illustrate through the course of this book, listening out for 'prescriptions for life' or discourses, as discussed in Chapter 3, is always important in understanding the cultural, social and political context in which someone's distress has developed. In Mary's case, this approach created space for conversations about the medicalisation of birth in the 1950s, ideas and scripts about 'motherhood', the expected roles of women and men, the stigma connected with mental health and how Mary's struggles were responded to by her then husband, services and society at the time. She experienced a sense of 'failure' coming out of hospital and not being able to 'cope' with the roles of a woman, wife and mother. Mary went on to talk in some depth about the experience of giving birth to her daughter and the parts that made this a trauma for her. A shift in the narrative occurred from what is wrong with you to what has happened to you (Johnstone and Boyle 2018). Mary could talk with self-compassion about attempts to achieve her own death and being taken into hospital.

Sadly, people's access to alternative, more positive stories in the face of 'problem-saturated' lives may be diminished by the ageing process, especially if loved ones have died. So, not surprisingly, many of the ideas and practices we use, such as club of life, re-membering and re-authoring, have already been described in the previous chapter on loss.

In the stories that follow, you will see how Jane and Rosslyn work with Joan, Jackie and Viv to use these practices to draw out stories that connect them to significant people in their life, whose perspectives can assist them in this therapeutic process.

Joan and re-membering conversations
Jane

When I first met Joan, she was struggling with the effects depression was having on her life, including negative opinions of herself and suicidal thoughts. Now in her 80s, she held on tightly to a narrative that she had been a 'bad mother' and that currently whatever she tried to do, she would do wrong, and others would suffer.

These narratives of blame, guilt and failure made it difficult for Joan to see herself in a way she would like to (her preferred identity). Her narrative about getting older was that, as she had lost her independence, she would quickly be put in 'the old lady box', which terrified her. In Chapter 3, we have referred to the ways in which ideas about how women and men 'should be' can be a big part of how people evaluate themselves in life.

Memories of past childhood trauma had reappeared in Joan's life following a stroke, meaning that she needed to be more dependent on others. There is a discourse or idea about trauma we hear a lot in our work, which is that people need to talk about everything in detail to feel better, and this influenced Joan. I began by attempting to create a sense of safety in our conversation. I was informed by an idea of 'standing together on a riverbank'.

> **STANDING ON THE RIVERBANK**
>
> Standing together on the riverbank is a concept discussed by Kaseke (2010), who highlights that by externalising a problem (separating it from oneself, as explained in Chapter 2), people can be supported to stand by the 'side of the river' and look on to the problem story in a different way. We find this an extremely valuable concept when thinking about how to find a stable standpoint from which to begin the telling of often very distressing stories. Preparatory work can sometimes be helpful with teams before therapy begins, which might include mapping out the riverbank and locating a safer, firmer place to stand. This can then be explored in therapy, fleshing out a subject which creates a sense of safety before more difficult subjects are broached.

I first listened to Joan's expression of what troubled her in her life. As discussed in Chapter 2, the idea of the 'absent but implicit' helps us to listen out for the values or hopes for life that might lie behind someone's emotional response. I had a sense that something important to her was being violated in some way and asked Joan what she was taking a stand against in showing this distress. I heard her upset and anger about the violence that had been in her family for generations and how powerless she had felt to stop it. She began to tell me about actions that she had taken which she came to name as 'Changing What's Expected about Violence in my Family'. In naming her commitment to this, a new narrative of self could begin to be richly described and, importantly, witnessed.

We began to list all the actions involved in this: 'Changing the Stories about Violence'. I discovered that Joan was teaching her grandchildren how to show what she called 'small acts of kindness'. She also talked about her great aunty, who provided the one loving relationship she had had as a child. We talked about all the ways she had provided small acts of love, such as giving her a much-needed plate of warm food and a feeling of being safe while they played. As we spoke about this, Joan said, 'Oh, I'm doing this now, I'm doing the aunty and grandma role'. I then asked her, 'What might you have contributed to the lives of your grandchildren? What might it have been like for them to experience this connection with you?' In considering what the small acts of kindness might mean to her grandchildren, she was able to think about herself in a more positive way, affirming her preferred identity.

I was really struck by how using these re-membering conversations about Joan's aunty had enabled us to move away from negative problem talk to a feeling of hope, commitment and a preferred identity which meant so very much. From the riverbank position of being the grandma who continues the acts of love, we were able to look at the thing that caused Joan so much pain: seeing herself as a 'bad mother'. We were able to lessen the power of and bring some compassion to the unhelpful narratives. I asked Joan, 'What could be possible if you held close being an influential grandma? What might your next steps be? How can you keep your aunty more present in your life now?' Soon after, Joan put a framed photograph of her and her aunty on the wall. I asked Joan what she thought her aunty would make of how she was living her life, her commitments and how she had kept her close. Joan thought she would be proud of her strength and not giving up and how she has continued to care so deeply for others.

Jackie and externalising responses to trauma
Jane

Jackie was referred to me following the sudden, unexpected death of her husband. The loss had triggered previous traumas to come tumbling into her life. Jackie was finding it very difficult to be in the home where she and her husband had lived together. Her husband had been her carer, and so she was now unable to get out of the house independently, leaving her feeling physically and emotionally trapped.

When we met and talked about what Jackie needed, we agreed that it did not feel like the right time to be looking into her past trauma in any depth. I felt that drawing on narrative principles of working with trauma, particularly responses to trauma, would be useful while Jackie felt so helpless waiting for alternative accommodation. We therefore talked about how, as a child, she climbed onto a roof in response to her father's violence and shouted out about what he had done to her. She also escaped and reported him at the police station. In response to him not letting her go to school, she put herself through college and became a manager.

In response to the traumatic loss of her first husband, she talked about the ways she rebuilt her life. Her current response to losing her husband was to take on things that she had not done before, such as sorting out paperwork and getting a mobile phone. When I enquired if there was a name that Jackie could call these responses, she replied, 'It's like a lion inside of me. After such awful experiences I have broken into a million of pieces, but then somehow got up and become stronger'. We both had a real sense of the lion roaring from the rooftop when she was a child.

In thinking about the lion as a response to trauma we were able to tap into its wisdom. Jackie knew that it did not feel safe to begin grieving for her husband while living in their home. We had a new understanding of why it was so difficult to return home: Jackie was having to work hard to put those grief feelings on hold. Jackie used a visual image of the lion when she arrived back home to keep close the value of strength inside of her. There seemed to be comfort in the knowledge that she will grieve one day but that it is okay for that not to be now. As we were saying goodbye after this conversation Jackie turned to me and said, 'That was really good today, wasn't it? It's made me know I can do it and I'm going to start writing again'. The next time I saw Jackie, she had a notebook with a picture of a lion on it and had started writing.

This work with Jackie reminds me of the power of externalising people's responses. As Angel Yuen (2009, p.9) says:

> What can be made possible when we are actively curious about how a person has responded to trauma, rather than only focusing on how they were affected by it?
>
> A response perhaps likely to be unnoticed or rendered insignificant could turn out to be a small gem of hope among the person's skills in living, cherished values, clever initiatives, and preferred ways of being.

How narrative conversations can assist people living with dementia and trauma
Rosslyn

From early in my career, the difficulties encountered by people living with dementia haunted by earlier traumatic memories had troubled me. Typically, the situation is something like this: a person finds that, as their cognitive abilities change, they notice that thoughts relating to earlier life events intrude more and become increasingly distressing. Triggers in their environment might lead them to believe that they are back in the traumatic situation from many years before. For a long time, there was very little published work in this area to guide me, so I started to draw on narrative practice in an attempt to find a way forward.

As we have discussed at the start of this chapter, re-emergence of early trauma can sometimes occur with cognitive change. In part, this may be due to difficulties in managing these memories, and it may also be that, where people struggle to form new memories and more recent memories are gradually eroded (as with Alzheimer's disease, for example), people will often revert to stronger memories, which are those that go back to earlier life (e.g. Koppel and Ruben 2016). As we have also mentioned, the psychological and emotional impact of dementia may trigger emotional states associated with trauma – for example, a sense of vulnerability or loss of control.

Early on in my journey in narrative practice, I worked with a woman recently diagnosed with Alzheimer's disease. She was experiencing many changes in her life, and her family struggled with what they experienced as aggression when they tried to assist her. She helped me to understand how much her ability to look after herself mattered to her – she had survived multiple traumas in her childhood and early adult life and prided herself on what she had overcome. She was now being subjected to terrifying nightmares relating to her childhood. I invited her to tell me about the ways in which she had come through her experience and built a life of which she was rightly proud. There continued to be challenges around her refusal to accept assistance, but this could be better understood. And what fascinated me was that the nightmares stopped.

Poh Lin Lee's (2013) paper 'Making Now Precious' held particular resonance for me, as it explains how we might make a difference by working in the here and now and what is possible in the moment. In Lin Lee's context, this is an asylum centre, where she may see someone only once. In my context, I think of the need to work with someone in the present, as they may often not remember the conversation that has gone before. Narrative practice enables us to work with the skills of people living with dementia – telling stories that are accessible and possible to remember.

Over the years in working in a community memory team, my colleagues and I have often been asked to support people struggling with distress during or after their diagnosis of dementia. The requests made to us as psychology practitioners rarely seem to be about trauma at the beginning. Rather, someone is anxious about the diagnostic process or distressed by their diagnosis. This was the case for Viv.

Viv and I would like to share the story of our work together. Viv has generously agreed to share her story as she feels that doing so could help others. She had always intended to write a book about her life, which she had wanted to call 'I'm a Survivor'. In her words, 'I'm doing this so that other people can see that there is a happy ending. There is help for everyone'.

I first met Viv when a medical colleague asked our psychology team to assist her with her anxiety, which was affecting Viv's ability to proceed with a memory assessment. Viv met with my colleague, Jazz, and let her know that her anxiety was due to a fear that she may have dementia. It wasn't dementia in itself that frightened Viv, but the thought of dying. In death, she feared meeting her late stepfather, who had abused her as a child. This early piece of work led to Viv sharing her experiences with her partner and daughter. Viv and Jazz worked on ways to manage her anxiety; she went ahead with her memory assessment and for a year or two Viv felt able to cope well with her day-to-day life and dementia diagnosis. However, following the death of her sister, she found that her anxiety came back, and she started to struggle more with nightmares and distressing memories. She therefore requested more psychological therapy, and at this point we met one another. Viv explained to me how close she and her sister had been. She feared for her sister's safety in the afterlife and was troubled by nightmares.

> **Viv**
> Throughout my periods of coming up to the hospital, it's been a slow, slow process. I feel that this last little spell has put a cap on it. Given me closure on all the nasties that happened to me as a youngster. It's helped me to feel more accepting of it all. Before I used to put it to the back of my mind but it kept popping up, but now it's like I can put a lid on it.
>
> I tried to tell people before, but I got a bad reaction from the teacher who said, 'Don't do that. You don't bring home life into the classroom,' and I could hardly look at her after that. It was the same with the doctor I tried to tell.
>
> Looking back, it would have been easy to end my life at that point. It's [narrative therapy] made me feel a bit more relaxed about the way I can look back. It's not so sharp that I'm reliving it. It's never going to go away. It was years and years ago, but sometimes years make no difference.
>
> The threat of him up there.
>
> As a youngster I decided that I wanted to help children. When I got ill (from not eating), I was sent to a convalescence place and their kindness there meant so much. I can still picture all the staff. One of them used to sneak me a biscuit, which I'd share with my friend.
>
> I learned to watch clouds. I remember sitting on the steps outside my flat when I left home watching the clouds, thinking 'This is nice'. I started with my sister. We would lie on the grass in the park, and I remember laughing uncontrollably at her. She would say, 'It's an elephant, there it is, that's its trunk'. That was our moment. It gave us strength as kiddies. You

wouldn't believe you could get strength from seeing the clouds. It's like an escape thing. You can go out into the garden and get lost.

There is something about speaking the stories out loud that helped me make sense. It's nothing you can see but I can feel the change in me. It's like an inner peace, as if I'm settling down at last over the years. I now have a sense of peace for my sister and a sense of safety for her. Before, I always felt he was up there and waiting. I remember saying to her, 'If you see him, don't forget you punch his lights out'. She would say, 'Yeah... And I'll stamp on him'. We'd joke that we would need a strong cloud. The hate that has always been there was like a big, dark blob, but slowly it is starting to separate. Bits are breaking off. It's getting smaller and smaller and fading away. It's actually working, and I never thought this could happen.

Rosslyn

I worked on the basis that one way to diminish the threat of Viv's stepfather might be to help Viv thicken and strengthen stories of the ways in which she tried to oppose him and to break free of him. Talking about her relationship with her sister seemed fundamental to this, and I therefore invited Viv to tell me lots of stories about this. This involved asking her to describe her sister and their relationship vividly – for example: 'What did she look like? How did she react when this happened? What do you remember doing together? Tell me more about the park where you used to go. Was it far from your house? Were there many trees? What did the grass feel like when you lay down in the park?' and so on. I drew on questions from re-membering practices to help with this such as, 'What did your sister think about this? What do you think she would say if she heard you say this now?'

Another part of Viv's story of breaking free was her courage and tenacity in leaving home at 16 and her determination to set up her own life, although this required her to manage on very little, to the extent that at times she had to shoplift in order to survive. In our conversations about this, I encouraged Viv to tell me about the skills she developed and the determination and hopes for a better life that lay behind these, such as: 'How did you know that children deserved to be cared for? Where did you learn this? Who let you know that you deserved a better life? How did they let you know this? How did you find the courage to leave home?'

RE-AUTHORING CONVERSATIONS
I tried to assist Viv to strengthen and thicken the stories that reminded her of her preferred identities in coping with life, finding strength, and deserving love and care by using re-authoring conversations. This is explained in Chapter 2 and refers to a process of mapping out similar stories at different times in someone's life, demonstrating continuity in their commitment to preferred values and identities, even when this might have become obscured.

Viv
My sister gave me an inner strength to cope with this rubbish, but when people's reactions are to judge, you lose confidence. She was one of those special people – protective and happy when others are happy – and very unassuming. She was my survival. I can talk about her, and I can't to everyone. It feels lovely to revisit memories of going to the park. I can go back there – feel the warmth and feel floaty and relaxed. I can feel the love. It was always such a strong tie. I couldn't have wished for a better sister – to talk to, to go with. She was so generous with her time and her company. She helped me out of many a pickle. When I was in digs, I only had enough for the bare essentials and didn't have money for everything I needed. I would go on a long bus ride to the Salvation Army so that people locally didn't see me. I got crafty with shoplifting, popping in when I could see they were busy with a delivery.

Rosslyn
I am hopeful that the process of retelling and 'thickening' stories of survival, love, connection and resistance has made these alternative narratives more present and accessible to Viv. This process appears to have diminished the threat of her stepfather. She tells me that the nightmares

occur much less often, and she has a sense of peace for her sister, who she now feels is safe. I hope that these other memories remain vivid for Viv. But we have talked together about ways that might help to ensure that she is able to hold on to them, being unsure how easy this will be for her as her dementia progresses. Viv had the idea of creating a book and perhaps asking her granddaughter to decorate her stories for her.

In Chapter 2, we reference the use of therapeutic documents, which can help us to share or document stories in ways that will be helpful. Newman (2008) speaks about 'rescuing the said from the saying of it'. The idea is that when small gems of hope are 'rescued' and used in a document of some kind, they can be 'held up' and enable the rich description to be put into 'circulation'. That is, the story can be shared and re-read (with the person's permission) by significant others over time. This can help to further thicken the alternative story.

In the box below is an example of a story that Viv has selected to share.

VIV'S STORY

When I left home I had my own little patch – my own room. I loved it. I knew I could close my door, and it wouldn't open. There was a scullery with an outside door leading down to the shared garden. There was a space at the top of the stairs where I could put a chair and sit in the sun. It was lovely. It was mine. I felt so proud of myself living there. I was only earning £5 a week and my rent was £3, but I had my bus fares and I bought some food. I used to pinch the odd apple or banana. I became a little tea-leaf, just for things to survive.

As you will see in Chapter 8, working with life stories need not always be in a clinical context of people accessing formal help for their distress. For people living with dementia generally, creative 'life story work' rooted in narrative practice can help to thicken preferred identities and stories of older people, especially if they are key in writing about themselves (Kaiser and Eley 2017). As someone living with dementia explained:

> It's fine at the moment, but it might get to the stage when I find it more difficult to express myself. I will want to make sure that people know about the things that have happened in my life...and maybe see me as more than the old lady in the corner. (Milton 2017, p.100)

Viv has some final thoughts about the process of therapy and what it has meant to her:

> You can come out of it. I don't think you're aware you're doing it until sometime later when you do it. I didn't used to be able to talk to anyone I didn't know. I used to stutter. Now I feel I can hold my own. It's surprising how it affects feeling, like the way you can relax. I was always fiddling with something. Some of the early part [of therapy] was upsetting. It opened a lid on a dark cloud, but it comes out into the light and you see a cloud with a silver edge.

We hope that this chapter has increased your curiosity to listen with and to older people's stories and to encourage witnessing and noticing the often-seen-and-not-heard stories of responses to trauma.

INVITATION TO REFLECT

- What do you think about this way of working with trauma, which places the emphasis on the person's response rather than the trauma itself?
- Was there anything in the stories we shared that resonated for you?
- How are you getting on with the narrative ideas that we have been building on over these initial chapters? Are they making sense? How do they fit with your ideas and values?

Useful resources

Denborough, D. (ed) (2006) *Trauma: Narrative responses to therapeutic experience*. Adelaide, Dulwich Centre Publications.

Johnstone, L. & Boyle, M. with Cromby, J., Dillon, J., Harper, D., Kinderman, P., Longden, E., Pilgrim, D & Read, J. (2018) *Power Threat Meaning Framework: Towards the identification of patterns in emotional distress, unusual experiences and troubled or troubling behaviour, as an alternative to functional psychiatric diagnosis.* Leicester, British Psychological Society.

Lin Lee, P. (2013) 'Making now precious: Working with survivors of torture and asylum seekers'. *International Journal of Narrative Therapy and Community Work 1*, 1–11.

Yuen, A. (2009) 'Less pain, more gain: Explorations of responses versus effects when working with the consequences of trauma'. *Explorations: An E-Journal of Narrative Practice 1*, 1–16. www.dulwichcentre.com.au/explorations-2009-1-angel-yuen.pdf

CHAPTER 6

What Does It Feel Like to Experience Narrative Therapy?

USING NARRATIVE THERAPY TO HELP NAVIGATE THE JOURNEY IN BECOMING A DEMENTIA CARE PARTNER

Rosslyn Offord and Karen Gibbs

We, Karen and Rosslyn, have known each other through the Cardiff and Vale Young Onset Dementia team for several years. We met initially when Karen's husband, Nick, requested help following his diagnosis of Alzheimer's disease at the age of 55 and asked if there might be any support for Karen.

We have worked together in different ways, reflecting the different needs Karen has had as her and Nick's situation evolved and changed. More recently, we have reflected on what it has been like to work using a narrative therapy approach. We share a passion for improving the care of people living with dementia and their supporters. Rosslyn has talked with Karen about the lack of research and literature relating to using this approach in dementia care, and together we felt we could play a part in improving this by sharing our experience with others.

In this chapter, we hope to share our experience of using narrative therapy in a way that assists both supporters/carers and clinicians in understanding both how this approach works and how it can be helpful. We also hope it might be helpful to people living with dementia, who may be looking for ways to support themselves in connecting to helpful stories of identity, as well those who support them.

We thought it would be helpful to discuss the following:

- How it felt to Karen being offered psychological therapy and what helped her to get started.
- Some of the emotional and psychological aspects of being a carer of someone living with dementia.
- What using narrative therapy looks like.
- What it is about narrative therapy that might be particularly helpful to carers of people living with dementia.

First, a note about terminology. We recognise that people caring for someone living with dementia and people living with dementia have different preferences for the term we use to describe the person in the caring role. Karen uses the word 'carer', so we will use this term in this chapter.

Getting started with narrative therapy
Karen

It was Nick who requested support from psychology initially. He had a sense that this would be helpful. At that time, he was still working and we couldn't be open about his diagnosis. Nick was getting support as a patient, and I was included alongside him, but I wasn't offered this personally. He asked: 'Is there something you could do for Karen?'

I knew I needed something. When you're a carer you're still mentally okay, but the person with dementia isn't and you automatically take on the care and support of them. At the same time, you're trying to feel your way through this forest of the unknown – What's ahead? What's around? No one could tell me how long it's going to last, and it's so difficult to understand the condition itself. This made it difficult to work out how I could accept this diagnosis, what it is, how should we tell people and so on. There is a stigma around dementia, especially at 55. People don't know how to approach it, especially when no one can tell you what the outlook is. All you know is that someone has pulled the rug from under your feet, and you are struggling in a very isolated way.

Although I knew I needed something, I didn't know where to find it. The literature isn't very helpful. It tells you about all the practical things, but what I needed was help in coming to terms with those deep emotions, and I had no idea what that would look like. In our case, it felt unhelpful that the literature is mostly written for people diagnosed in older age, which added to the sense of stigma. I had received an appointment on formal NHS paper inviting Nick and me to an appointment with a psychologist, but I was thinking, 'What are we going to? Are we going to be labelled?' It's slightly unnerving to get NHS letters anyway, then there's the stigma about psychology and psychiatry too. In the back of my mind, there was all this American stuff about 'going to see my shrink' and lying on a couch. I went not knowing if it was a test or not. Someone like me has no idea of what psychology is or how it can help.

We went to a strange little room, and it did feel odd for a while. However, Rosslyn explained things. She and her colleague were welcoming and kind, and I realised this was not an inquisition. They helped me to understand the safety of talking with them. I understood that our conversations would be confidential, and I could see that they were professional, well-trained and sympathetic. I could feel that they were not going to be judgemental. I understood from them that this was support for me rather than any kind of medical intervention.

What using narrative therapy looks like
Karen

At the beginning, what helped was a psycho-educational course for dementia carers called START (STrAtegies for RelaTives programme; Livingston et al. 2019). It helped me to know I was being given something solid that had been developed by University College London. There were helpful suggestions in each unit, and I felt as if I was learning. Doing an individualised course, where I could talk about my experiences in this structured way with a trainee psychologist, was helpful in the first instance, as I could get used to the idea of opening up and feeling comfortable with someone else in the room. It was helpful for me to be able to see the development in my understanding over time. It helped me to learn strategies, especially around relaxation and mindfulness. For me that was a really good introduction.

For a while, I was able to use the strategies I had learned with START to carry on caring for Nick, and that felt like enough. However, over time, the doctor realised I could do with a bit more help. She would meet Nick and me every 6 months for a review and arranged to have some one-to-one time so that I could speak openly. She asked how I was coping with life at home. I found it quite emotional, and when she asked if some further psychological support would help, I knew that it would. Although I had done the START course with psychology before, I didn't know I could ask for it. I'm not sure I would have asked for it if I'd realised it was available. Maybe I would have done, but I was brought up to cope if you can. There was a sense for me that I didn't feel I deserved it: I know how stretched the NHS is, and Nick is the patient, not me.

What using narrative therapy has been like
Karen

Your full-time caring commitment leaves you very little room to think too much about yourself, but actually it's very important to give yourself some time. It's difficult to find and there's so much to do. This hour I have, now just every couple of months, is reassuring. It's just for the carer, it's not for the person you're caring for. It's an hour just to spend on yourself and come to terms with what you are really thinking and feeling. A lot of the time you are suppressing those thoughts in order to cope. This gives you a chance to let go of all those inhibitions and let the emotions flow. I can say why caring can feel so irritating or why it's so sad or terrible. I'm speaking to somebody who is a professional person, who isn't just a friend and who isn't going to judge me. Rosslyn is there to support me rather than say, 'Why don't you do this or that?' or 'I know'. You have a listener for yourself for an hour who is actually helpful in asking questions to allow you to explore your own thoughts and own ways of managing. By the end of an hour, I feel like my situation is clarified each time. I feel quite drained, but I feel I can carry on. I can continue. I feel like I have been helped to get to grips with the emotional reality of the situation and its life-changing effect.

Rosslyn

One of the things that got me thinking about writing this with Karen was a comment she made at the end of one of our sessions when she said, 'You ask the right questions'. I remember trying to explain that the questions came from her. This is where narrative practice feels so helpful and feels different to other approaches I have been trained to use.

> When I first did my narrative training, I recall the surprise at hearing that 'Wherever your conversation gets to should be unexpected'. As psychologists, our usual approach is to formulate what you think the problem is and hypothesise as to what will be helpful for the person you are working with, guiding them through sessions to get there. In narrative therapy, we are trained to resist hypothesising. As we discussed in Chapter 2, there is an idea that we assist someone to move from what is 'known and familiar' (the well-told narratives) to the 'possible to know'. We do this by listening very carefully, perhaps for exceptions to the problem situation, perhaps for discourses that might be leading someone to feel stuck, perhaps for something that is implied but not said explicitly. These are all things that can be available for the person to think more about but may not be fully evident to them in that moment – 'possible to know'. So, when I ask Karen 'the right questions' I am delighted. I do not start out with a plan or idea as to what those questions will be, but if they feel right, it's because I have managed to hear what she needs me to.

On many occasions, I will hear a range of possible things I could ask about. For example, I might say something like, 'I'm interested in asking you more about what you think about staying at home more, but I'm also wondering about this issue of feeling guilty. Which feels most relevant to you at the moment to talk about? What do you think is more important today?'

Karen

When I come to the sessions, I often have very little idea of what I need to discuss. It has seemed to me that sessions are much more structured, that Rosslyn had some kind of plan or knew where we were going. At the end it feels like there's been a plan. I feel, 'That's spot on; that's what I need'.

Rosslyn

Although I do not follow a plan for what we will talk about, I do use a structure to help frame our conversations, using Michael White's (2007) 'maps', as explained in Chapter 2, to guide our conversations. This helps me to follow some of the key principles of narrative therapy we have discussed, such as encouraging rich, detailed storytelling about the situation and assisting Karen to name and externalise a particular problem. This can also help her to establish her position on a challenging situation, as we can discuss why Karen may feel the way that she does by considering the situation in the context of her values and her family and social environment. From my perspective in working with carers, the ability that narrative therapy gives me to consider the wider 'social discourses', as discussed in Chapter 3, feels important and distinctive about this approach. There are frequently ideas around duty, or expectations about caring, relationships and different roles, which are linked with things such as gender, class, culture and religion, which can often be helpful for people to notice and give thought to.

Karen and I have spent time thinking about this in various ways. For example, Karen has often shared a sense of failure about not 'doing more' in relation to social activities and engagements. Both she and Nick lived busy lives before dementia. She has noticed that the times Nick and her are happiest together is at home, maybe sitting in the garden or listening to music. Despite having learned from Nick that taking things more slowly and keeping to a routine works better, she has still had times when she has doubted herself, wondering if she should be 'trying harder'. There has been a nagging doubt that perhaps she is being a bit lazy or 'staying too much within her comfort zone'.

I have understood that there can be different pressures here. One is the 'use it or lose it' idea, which gets Karen worrying that maybe she is not providing enough stimulation for Nick. Another seems to be around 'living life to the full', 'making the most out of life', which seemed to connect with discourses in her social group about how retirement should be, as well as wider social discourses connected to coming out of the pandemic. These created a sense of pressure for Karen that she should be doing more – travelling, social engagements and so on. Having a way to tease out where these ideas come from has felt important. In doing this, Karen has had space to consider what she feels about these ideas, and how they might fit with the values and preferences she holds for her life and for Nick's.

There have been some discourses, such as the importance of learning, that fit for Karen. Together, we have traced the history of this in Karen's life, linking it to family values and her choice of career as a teacher. At an earlier point in our work, she was able to see pursuing opportunities for learning as something she could think differently about. She and Nick were learning to dance together and that could be enough. More recently, however, as time passes and Nick is less able to join Karen in learning new dance steps, we have returned to this. While it did not feel right for Karen to pursue her own interests and learning at an earlier stage, when Nick was more able to join her in activities, this has changed. Using a narrative framework for our conversations has assisted me in finding ways to help Karen 'deconstruct' or think about the different factors that influence her thinking and decision-making about this, to weigh and consider them, and to go on to identify a way forward for herself.

Karen

These conversations clarified the current situation and 'gave permission' for me not to have to strive for more in the current situation and the confidence to go forward in these different ways.

How narrative therapy helps
Karen

'Living well' and being positive is great for the person living with dementia. Nick has always been very sociable, and he can participate in groups and activities that are offered to him. But for the carer, you're in a dementia world and you don't have dementia. So, actually, living well is quite a false way of life for the carer. It's a way of life that you have to accept. It's as if you have been given crutches; you have to take on the dementia yourself in order to enable the person you care for to live well with it. For example, we joined a trip to Porthcawl recently; it was lovely, and I embraced it, but I had felt, 'I want a trip to Paris or London'. Of course, the dementia world can help me as a carer too; you form a parallel world that you can become quite comfortable in, but the carer has another life that mustn't be ignored and that can be difficult to find.

It is easy to be consumed by this one aspect of identity – 'the carer' – when previously you have enjoyed a range of diverse roles – wife, mother, professional, social roles. You have to be aware that you are losing some of these aspects of yourself in order to preserve the ones that you feel you need to be recognised for now. Just having a chance to talk and express myself to Rosslyn, an unbiased professional, helps me to understand how my sense of self is affected by the (passive) dementia, now that Nick is no longer able to hold a conversation with me in the same way as we had previously enjoyed. Just the chance every few weeks to speak and express my identity helps. I appreciate being asked what it's like to try and untangle the different pressures on how I should be managing – what do I really feel and what do I want to do? – and to pinpoint what the external pressure actually is. This often helps me to let go of the things now that I just can't do and provides the means to explore how relevant those roles I can no longer fulfil are.

An illustration of this loss of opportunity are the plans Nick and I had for the time when the children were off our hands. We had hoped to spend weekends away to enjoy our interests, such as going to the theatre, visiting galleries, trying new restaurants and so on; we were looking forward to a more relaxed social life. This is no longer possible at this stage in Nick's dementia as any outing requires thorough planning and risk assessment. The fact that life has become so restricted for me is a grief in itself. I experience a huge sense of loss. The fact that our friends and family are enjoying the lifestyle we had looked forward to only exaggerates this sense of sadness and frustration.

The misguided advice I often receive from others in their attempts to be helpful in encouraging me to participate more only adds to the problem. The therapy sessions provide huge support in dealing with these emotions and pressures. I am offered the opportunity to explore the activities that I feel are currently denied to me. I can allow them to be put on hold for the time being rather than letting go completely. This helps me to manage the frustration of not being able to live the way I would like to. It also gives me the space to appreciate the rather alternative life I find myself leading and enrich it with a range of experiences that are still accessible to both Nick and me, as well as developing hobbies for myself which can be fitted around my caring responsibilities.

Another example of the grief of not being able to fulfil a role I care so much about is the time when my eldest daughter had her baby, and I couldn't go to visit and support her just after the birth. I felt overwhelmingly angry that I could not fulfil my role as mother and grandmother. I felt entirely trapped by my circumstances. Nick could not understand. It was a very difficult time for me. My youngest daughter was able to be with her sister and did a fantastic job. It actually had no consequence that I was not there, as both daughters were highly competent and both understood entirely why I was not able to help. However, I found it extremely difficult that I could not provide the support I longed to offer or to share at first hand the joy of a new baby. It was very helpful to speak about the resentment with Rosslyn. It helped me to deal with those feelings of frustration due to the incapacity to act, the anger and the grief. By putting it all into perspective through our discussions, I was able to come to terms with the situation and to banish the blame I had put upon Nick.

For me, being able to talk in this way is a release. You can experience that in other ways, like watching a sad movie or going for a long walk. It's almost like a physical way of dealing with those emotions. Because it's a huge sadness to watch someone go through dementia; it's grief every day. It doesn't change things dramatically, but I feel refreshed and ready to carry on and continue. On the whole, I have to suppress the grief in order to maintain normality, but it doesn't go away; it's there and you can't deny it. And those sessions allow you to acknowledge it and say, 'Yes, this is terrible'. I feel a sense of well-being from having taken the lid off. Everything is calm afterwards. Without the opportunity to talk with Rosslyn, I would feel a lot more frustration and anger and a sense of entrapment. If I didn't have time to explore these feelings, I wouldn't be able to stay calm. There are times when I do lose my temper, but it doesn't happen very often. Without this, I think I would be overcome by that a lot more, and that would certainly affect Nick. He becomes defensive if I'm angry and this creates conflict. If I can remain calm, it keeps the situation manageable and more enjoyable for him. If he picks up my frustration or sadness, he can become anxious and can't understand, and that can create other conflicting emotions, as I still have the anger but it's due to grief.

Without this therapy, it would be harder for Nick and me to go forward together. This applies to managing my anger and frustration but also my grief. Grief is always there and doesn't go away, but I can't give in to it with Nick as I don't want to create a sad or depressed atmosphere; I want to maintain a warm and comfortable relationship. This grief has to be acknowledged, and it can be managed in the sessions. Sometimes, there can be a day or two when it can feel overwhelming, and I can feel like I can't go forward. Being able to talk about it provides a strategy to accept it, give in to it sometimes and then find positive aspects to our relationship. Although grief is always there, there's still a lot of enjoyment that can be found. And sometimes you have to laugh and see the funny side of it all.

I don't go in knowing what I'm going to talk about; this is the weird thing, except when there is something very practical and very physical. On one occasion there was a practical side – toileting issues – which was upsetting for me. And it helped that Rosslyn is part of the team caring for Nick as there is practical backup there as well; I know she would put me in touch with the right person if that's needed. So, it's different to an anonymous psychologist who doesn't know the background, and there is a trust that comes from Rosslyn being part of the team, which also helps. In that instance, I needed to be able to talk about my horror about managing toileting but also the practicalities. This situation was an example of me finding I could cope with something I thought I couldn't, and therapy helped me through that. Now I can look back and see how I adapted. I still don't know how I will cope in the future; I just think about the present. The sessions help me concentrate on this, along with the grounding and the mindfulness I learned from the START course.

Rosslyn

I think Karen makes an important point here about how using narrative therapy fits within the broader service context in which we work. The philosophy of narrative therapy is one which places the person and their knowledge of what they need at the centre. If then at a particular point in time, what that person needs to do is to step outside of more reflective work and to think through some practical strategies, this is possible. What is important is to talk explicitly about what the person needs at that moment and to offer some ideas that can be talked about, while acknowledging that this may mean a bit of a gear change or different type of conversation. Strategies that I have offered to Karen, such as in the toileting situation she references here, are shared in the spirit of collaboration rather than expertise – for example, 'I've found that other carers have found this idea helpful. Would you like to hear more about it?' This feels like an important difference from advice-giving. Karen's reflection additionally helps me to understand the value of coming to this work as part of a multidisciplinary team and as a therapist who also has knowledge and experience specific to dementia care that I am able to share, as opposed to seeing a generic therapist in a mental health or primary care setting.

So often, I find that care partners bring to me a dilemma about managing their own needs alongside those of the person they care for. Narrative therapy has helped me to find ways to fully explore the nature of these needs in a different way. Rather than stopping at personal preferences or taking the idea of needs at face value, it asks *why* these things might matter. We can ask for the stories in someone's life that help us to understand where those needs have come from. It feels that this is helpful in enabling someone to see that something they've always believed to be absolutely necessary, or a duty they have never questioned, is simply an idea that may or may not be true for them. It may or may not be something they want to continue with in their life. This can have the effect of liberating people from duties or responsibilities that may not have served them well. On the flip side, it can assist care partners to recognise the parts of their lives or identities that they may be neglecting and which may be therefore contributing to their distress.

For example, when Karen was able to work out that it was okay to let go of a full social calendar or attend cultural events with Nick, she felt freed up to enjoy the simple things that she and Nick were appreciating rather than feeling like she had failed by not being able to continue to live the lifestyle her friends enjoyed. On the other hand, these conversations can also help to strengthen people's commitment to what is important to them and assist in finding ways to make this possible. In Karen's case, her commitment to being someone who is learning new things has been important, and I have encouraged her to tell me stories about times when she has done this and what this has meant to her. In more traditional therapy, we might have identified some of these issues and weighed them up together. But we would not have deconstructed this in quite the same way, examining the social and cultural factors that influence how we feel about ourselves and others. There is also something about the telling of stories to illustrate these issues that enriches this work. As explained in Chapter 2, we use the idea of 'thickening', which refers to strengthening the preferred stories in our lives. We do this by looking for further stories, often buried in the past, and inviting them to be told in rich ways which help to illustrate the values we live by.

Karen

As a carer, what you might want to know is likely to be different depending on where you are on this journey. It gives you a chance to explore your own reactions to the diagnosis that has hit not only the person you are caring for but has affected you as well. So, it gives you the opportunity to explore all the emotions which surround that life-changing moment, when you know you are going to lose your best friend, the person you've relied on, and be the person they depend on. This kind of therapy helps you to transition from being a partner to becoming the person who has to take the initiative for that life together to continue. It also assists with the job of gradually taking on more responsibilities as the dementia progresses, in order to find a way forward together, while at the same time trying to preserve your own sense of self.

The fact that so many stories can be found in my life provides a strength in itself and enables me to accept the current situation. To accept this as a new story which provides some worthwhile and rich experience adds breadth and a reason to go forward.

INVITATION TO REFLECT

- Having read about Karen and Rosslyn's experience of using narrative therapy, do you have a sense of how it might feel or how it could be helpful to you or others?
- Is there anything about this approach that you feel drawn to or interested in? Why might that be?

Afterword
Rosslyn

Since writing this together, Karen and I joined a colleague to deliver some teaching for trainee clinical psychologists about narrative therapy. In this teaching, my colleague invited the two of us to reflect on the experience of working together using this approach. As I have come to expect from narrative conversations, this took me to a place I had not expected. I found myself considering a discourse about being able to make things better or 'fix' a difficult situation, which is often around for those of us working in healthcare. Karen turned to me in surprise and said, 'I never expected you to be able to fix the situation'. This particular moment in our conversation was striking to me and, it turned out, to the trainee psychologists listening. While the idea that we can fix things seems ridiculous on one level, it turns out that many of us working in therapy can find ourselves feeling subject to this expectation. It was very helpful to us to notice that this can be going on. For me, this example illustrates how helpful a narrative approach can be to us as therapists too.

Karen

Dementia brought about an episode in my life which froze my independence for 10 years. I struggled against a hurricane of emotions to find the ways and means to care for my husband and to preserve our relationship. At the time, the difficulties appeared endless, and the grief swelled full of love, anger and fear. Now, the most feared but most anticipated event has happened. Nick has passed away, and I am here without my husband and without dementia.

There is a sense of peace. The grief prevails but it is gentle and sad, no longer aggressive and overwhelming. It is clear to me that I could not have maintained the responsibility of Nick's care without the regular sessions with Rosslyn, in which we analysed my reactions to the horrors as they arose during the progress of Nick's dementia and found ways to accept and manage them. I am very grateful that I was able to care for Nick and sincerely believe that with the support of narrative therapy we lived the best life we could with dementia. I was able to talk openly about the issues I had in my changing relationship with my husband. I knew that I would not be judged or presented with futile advice. It was a chance for me to devote all my thoughts to my own emotions. I was encouraged to assess the turmoil I found myself in and found ways to untangle and address it, often by considering past events in my life or remembering people who have supported or influenced me. This helped me to understand what was most important to me at the time and to find a way forward which was totally acceptable to me. It helped me to appreciate the things that Nick and I could still do together: we could dance, take part in creative-arts-therapy activities, enjoy our dinner each evening with music that had always been meaningful to us, go for slow walks, sit in our garden and, above all, share time with our family. The narrative therapy sessions were completely draining emotionally, but they offered me a release from the tension which builds up in caring for someone with dementia. There was a much-needed emotional release. Afterwards, I felt positive and able to carry on. Narrative therapy helped us to do dementia our way.

CHAPTER 7

Working Alongside Service Users with Narrative Therapy Practices

Helen Carter

Setting the scene

I work in community mental health services for older people within the NHS in South-West England. The people I meet with express significant distress, may feel 'out of sorts' and frequently speak about loss – of people, of abilities and of themselves, and typically appear to struggle to enjoy or engage with life.

Several years ago, I noticed that the stories of hard times I was listening to were often being told in ways that were similar. They drew on familiar ways of understanding distress that were pathologising, individualising, blaming, limiting and isolating for the person. I could see that this had led people to come to 'thin' conclusions about themselves and the difficulties they were facing.

I used to think how amazing it would be if I could connect people to others who had previously consulted with me, as they too had once struggled through hard times. The aim of creating such a connection was to lessen feelings of difference, inadequacy and isolation, while passing a beacon of hope around. Stories of courage, abilities, qualities and skills that had been cultivated through adversity could be shared and authenticated with others. This would serve to amplify these skills and qualities, but also enhance the development of 'thicker', or stronger, identity conclusions as they continued on their journeys through life.

This chapter will outline the venture I took to fulfil this ambition of bringing people together. I will share how I have used the practices of definitional ceremony and of narrative documentation by letter-writing. These methodologies are easy to engage with while also offering rigorous, effective and hopeful approaches to responding to distress and adversity.

Some of the key principles of these practices include:

- Enabling people to tell their stories in ways that make them stronger.
- Enabling people to make a contribution to others who are also experiencing hard times.
- Recognising that the experience of making a contribution sustains and generates hope.
- Recognising that there is always more than one story.
- Recognising that people are always responding to the difficulties they are facing.

In outlining these principles, I am drawing on the work of Michael White and David Epston (1990), David Denborough (2008) and Angel Yuen (2009).

I will illustrate how working collaboratively with service users has been key to the successful development and implementation of these practices. I was privileged to be able to draw on the knowledge of our service-user engagement group, which consists of people who have accessed local mental health services.

What is definitional ceremony?

The concept of definitional ceremony is discussed by Michael White (1995), who drew on the work of the anthropologist Barbara Myerhoff in the 1980s, who is also referenced in relation to re-membering practices (see Chapter 4). Having studied how members of an elderly Jewish community attending a day centre in California told the stories of their lives, Myerhoff concluded that this opportunity to have their stories witnessed dealt with problems of invisibility and marginality.

She described the opportunities 'for being seen and in one's own terms, garnering witnesses to one's own worth, vitality, and being' (Myerhoff 1986, p.267).

Michael White (1995) brought this idea of definitional ceremony into his therapeutic work, with his methodology of 'outsider witness practice'. This provided a carefully orchestrated space for people to share stories that could be witnessed by an audience of one or more carefully chosen people, who are referred to as 'outsider witnesses'. It is the therapist's role to convene and facilitate a definitional ceremony session, and to prepare all participants in advance. It is important that the outsider witnesses act as an audience and do not join in or interrupt the telling of the story, just as the person at the centre should only listen and not join in when the outsider witnesses are interviewed. It is the therapist's job to hold these different positions and to also help the witnesses to avoid giving advice, but instead to stay close to reflecting and connecting with their own experience.

For those who are interested in knowing how to structure these sessions, please consult the text box below.

THE STRUCTURE OF A DEFINITIONAL CEREMONY SESSION (FROM WHITE 2007)

1. *The telling:* The person at the centre of the definitional ceremony begins with a 'telling' of their story to which the outsider witness(es) listen.

    The story is told to the therapist with the audience set apart. The therapist may talk with the person about their struggles with hard times, what actions they have been taking in response to their struggles, what skills and resources they have been drawing upon, and why it has been important for them to address these problems.

2. *The retelling:* A 'retelling' of the person's story is told by the outsider witness(es).

The service user here takes an audience position and listens to the conversation between the facilitator and the outsider witness. In this conversation, the facilitator poses four lines of enquiry:

a. *The expression:* What phrase or sentence were you drawn to? What stood out to you or struck a chord? What did you hear that they thought gave a sense of what the person accorded value to in life?

b. *The image:* Did an image come to mind while you were listening? *Note that the image is anticipated to be metaphorical and could represent something they have heard about the person's life or their identity.*

c. *Resonance:* What is it about your own experiences that meant this expression or image captured you?

d. *Transport:* Where has this experience moved you to that you might not have got to had you not witnessed this today? What might you now do on account of these new understandings?

3. *The retelling of the retellings:* Here, the focus moves back to the person at the centre of the conversation. This person now has the opportunity to reflect on what they have heard from the outsider witness. They, too, can be guided through the four lines of enquiry, although the emphasis remains on their life and identity rather than those of the outsider witness.

Interviewing the person at the centre of the definitional ceremony with these lines of enquiry enables the opportunity for rich story development. New possibilities are opened up regarding ways to address difficulties, as well as for connection and solidarity.

My journey into bringing definitional ceremony into my work

The process of collaborating with service users in bringing definitional ceremony into my practice began with my consulting with an ex-service user, who I will call Joe. I had previously met with Joe when he was referred to me in relation to worsening difficulties he was experiencing with anxiety. Joe had agreed for me to reach out to him following the conclusion of our sessions together. In talking with Joe, my enthusiasm for definitional ceremonies must have shone through. We were soon embarking on a practice session in which Laura, a trainee psychologist, joined us. In this session, Joe took the opportunity to be at the centre of the conversation, with Laura taking the outsider witness position. This enabled Joe to have the experience of being at the centre of a definitional ceremony session and to appreciate its value. The roles were then swapped between Laura and Joe, so that he could become familiar with the entire process.

From here, Joe volunteered to be an outsider witness for Thomas, who at the time was meeting with me for difficulties with which Joe was familiar. Thomas spoke positively of his experiences of the session and subsequently volunteered himself to be an outsider witness once his therapy sessions had concluded. Thomas then became an outsider witness in a session for Mark. Mark also found the session valuable and has subsequently expressed his desire to join my register of potential outsider witness contributors.

An illustration of a definitional ceremony session: Thomas's story

Thomas has kindly agreed that I can share his experience. He was joined by Joe as an outsider witness, as explained above. Thomas and Joe were both White English men aged in their 70s, both were retired and both had experience of having struggles with anxiety, albeit in quite different ways.

At the time of the session, Thomas had met with me a number of times. He had helped me to understand that he had been experiencing difficulties with anxiety since he was a child and had previously relied on others to help him cope; first his siblings and then his wife. His struggles had significantly worsened since his wife's death approximately 18 months prior.

As described above, I had met with both Thomas and Joe in order to prepare for the session. After brief introductions and a reminder of the structure of the session, a conversation commenced between Thomas and me, with Joe taking the position of outsider witness. This initial conversation offered an opportunity for Joe to hear about Thomas and some of his circumstances and responses. This included Thomas speaking of how anxiety comes in the evenings, making these very difficult times for him. Thomas then took the audience position, as I embarked on a conversation with Joe that followed the four lines of enquiry. Joe was asked, 'In listening to the conversation between Thomas and me, was there anything in particular that you were drawn to?'

In Joe's response, he referred to feeling the sadness in Thomas's account. He said that he did not find this surprising, given Thomas's recent losses of both his wife and his career since retiring. Joe referenced Thomas's courage in carrying on despite his losses. He also discussed the likely process of adjustment, and of the frustration in this process requiring time.

The following is the conversation that followed between Joe and me as we worked through the outside witness responses, as per the box above.

Helen: Did you have an image that came to mind that reflected any of those aspects that you talked about?

Joe: I was thinking about football. I see it like Thomas is a player in a football team and he's always had a manager, someone else always managing his life. But now the manager's left and they've elected Thomas to be the player manager, so Thomas has taken over as the manager now. This was a big shock for him, but with encouragement from his team, his family and his friends, he's accepting that he's now the manager.

Helen: And in that picture you have of Thomas as team manager, does it give you an idea of who Thomas is or what he might aspire to? Can you picture him as the team manager there?

Joe: Yeah, I mean I get the impression that he's worked all his life, he's always done well with work, so they're all positive things, and he's got his family around him as well. I know it's difficult when you're feeling wretched and you don't realise the support that you get, but he did mention that he had such a family like that, which is great. And I think that support from his family is going to help him win a promotion.

Helen: Joe, is there anything from your own experiences that made that image, or anything else from listening to Thomas, resonate for you or stand out for you?

Joe's responses included:

> As you know I've suffered with anxiety all my life as well, and I've had fears of being on my own and there's been times when I don't like being on my own, so it has struck a lot of resonance with me... You know it's difficult, like when you've been with somebody all your life, like I have, then being in that house on your own, and you walk in and it's empty, you know. It's just you who's got to do all the things in the house: you've got to cook and clean yourself, dress and do the housework; and sometimes for a man these things can be particularly difficult.

Joe spoke too of how he could also find it difficult to realise what resources he has during times of struggles.

On moving to the 'transport' question, I asked, 'And Joe, final question for you: what has it got you thinking about today having listened to Thomas? Has it got you thinking about how you might do anything differently?' Joe talked of how listening to Thomas had reminded him of his own self-care methods, particularly why he engaged with his volunteer work, which was to help with his boredom post-retirement, to provide a distraction, and 'that helping other people can sometimes get you out of yourself and stop you thinking of yourself so much'. The conversation also made Joe think of his own future, but with recognition that there was no point in worrying about this too much.

It was at this point that Joe resumed his audience position and the conversation restarted with Thomas:

Helen: Was there anything that struck you from what Joe said?
Thomas: Well, one thing that he is absolutely right on is the fact that I'm the manager now. That was a great thing for him to say because I've never thought of it like that, and it sort of honed in on me.

Our conversation continued around this football metaphor. This included a discussion of how his role as manager was quite a newly appointed role and how he was still learning the ropes. Thomas identified how anxiety – the opposing team – could be expected to try and score some goals against him at times, but how he had a good team to support him in his new role. I ended the session by asking Thomas: 'What's it been like having Joe in here today?' to which Thomas replied: 'I thought it was good because he was listening. The big thing was that… I've lost a manager (laughs). I thought that was a good way of describing it because that does sum up a lot, doesn't it?'

In following the outsider witness lines of enquiry, it felt important to be guided by Thomas's interest in the metaphor provided by Joe, and keeping the focus here seemed valuable in thickening this alternate, preferred identity for Thomas. In addition to the football metaphor, I was interested in references Joe made to his stage in life and to being a man. These features of Joe's identity are similar to Thomas's, and I wonder if these similarities assisted in creating a connection between the two men and their struggles.

The presence of the outsider witness appeared beneficial to both Thomas and Joe. Joe spoke of the benefit for him in being able to be helpful to somebody else, which has also been important to him in his volunteer work. Joe also emphasised the importance of hope, and hoped that his contributions in the session offered hope to Thomas. For Thomas, this session provided several opportunities for him: to be connected to somebody else who has experienced similar difficulties; to observe Joe's ability to manage anxiety; to have his distress witnessed and acknowledged as testimony to his love for his wife; and to have the opportunity for his preferred identity as a capable and competent person to be witnessed, recognised and accentuated.

How the definitional ceremony has been experienced: feedback from participants at the centre of the ceremony

I am often curious as to the effects of inviting ex-service users to be outsider witnesses for those who are at the centre of the conversation and for those in the position of outsider witness. I have subsequently interviewed different people who have taken the various positions involved in this practice, and they have been very willing to share their experiences and for their comments to be made available to others.

Overwhelmingly, those at the centre of the sessions speak positively about their experiences. In this, there is a recognition of the importance of being carefully listened to. As Newman (2008) identifies, we are dealing with the *meaning* of what people say, not just with what is said. Retellings that express an appreciation for the person's meaning are likely to contribute to rich descriptions and to a sense of feeling authentically heard. One person at the centre of a definitional ceremony spoke of how he felt very honoured by the outsider witness's retellings of his commitments, purposes, values and identity claims.

Linking stories around shared themes seems to offer opportunities to thicken preferred stories and of living one's life in ways that are personally valued, for participants at the centre of the conversation and the person in the outsider witness position. Joe's comments illustrate how being at the centre of the definitional ceremony enabled him to feel that his worth was witnessed and acknowledged:

> It certainly helps to reinforce the positives of who you are as a person, things that you might not necessarily see in yourself but other people see in you. It helps to develop you as a person, I think, having somebody else feed back to you about your good points…it just reinforces those strengths, that you know you can do those things and people are telling you, you know. It's important to have that feedback. It just makes you feel stronger about that, you can move forward.

As Myerhoff (1982, 1986) suggested, the active participation by the outsider witness in the retellings of Joe's accounts appeared important in validating the person he wanted to be. Joe also spoke of what this development made possible – 'that you can move forward'. This 'moving forward' speaks to White's (2002) use of the metaphor of 'katharsis'. This goes beyond the traditional meaning of 'catharsis' in psychology, referring to an experience of being transported to another place from which one, for instance, might have a new perspective, re-engage with neglected aspects of one's own history, initiate steps in one's life otherwise never considered, think beyond what one routinely thinks and so on.

James, another person who has participated in outsider witness practice, expressed his reaction at hearing that the outsider witness in his session had taken some influence from him:

> Well, that's compliment indeed if I was able to influence somebody... the first thing I met was this big guy up here whose hands buried mine, and for me to instil some motivation by what I was saying is...I didn't even realise. We have an individual who is obviously quite intelligent and well-educated who is in some way influenced by me. It's quite something, it really is... To hear that I could possibly have had some kind of influence on him – good, great. Really good, great. That's nice to know.

The surprising and rewarding effects for having taken part in a definitional ceremony session did not stop at the person who was at the centre of these sessions.

How the definitional ceremony was experienced: outsider witness responses

After acting as an outsider witness, Jeff talked about what it meant for him to be able to help somebody else: 'I feel like, "Oh, I've done something positive," you know, instead of feeling like I'm not able to do anything like that. I'm like, "Oh, I've done something I didn't think I was able to do," so yeah, it's great'. When I asked Jeff if he felt he had gained something from contributing to the session, he responded: 'Well, yes, I probably did, even being able to do it. A couple of years ago I thought, "You wouldn't be able to do anything like that; what are you talking about?" you know, but I can. So instead of "I can't" it's "I can", which is much better'.

Having undertaken the role of an outsider witness just once, new things appeared to be more possible for Jeff: he can offer something to somebody else, speak up, speak out about his own difficulties, be useful and be of value, be honest, be genuine and be seen on his own terms. The process also enabled Jeff's preferred expressions of identity to be witnessed and acknowledged.

SETTING UP DEFINITIONAL CEREMONIES: TOP TIPS
Tip 1: Keep a register of outsider witnesses

As referenced by Michael White (2007), I keep a list of people who have agreed to potentially work with me as an outsider witness. This means I have their consent to contact them once they have left the service. In growing the register, I have asked service users directly if this is something they may wish to consider offering to others in the future. People have also approached me to offer their assistance, such as trainees and members of the service-user engagement group, after hearing about this way of working – it appears that people are really enthused by the potential opportunity to offer something to others in this way!

Tip 2: Prepare both current therapy service users and outsider witnesses in advance

Sometimes, giving an outsider witness a practice session with a colleague can be helpful, so that they can experience how this will feel before deciding whether to proceed. It is also important to ensure that a full discussion is had about what the session involves and how it may feel, so that we can be sure service users and outsider witnesses are making an informed choice before consenting to involvement. Preparation additionally includes a discussion of expectations around confidentiality and an agreement is signed. Information sheets are given to participants to help with this preparation.

Tip 3: Ensure that outsider witnesses understand the process of staying in the listening position without joining in

Participants also need to be prepared to avoid getting into advice-giving, praising or judging the person they are witnessing. This is explained in more detail in an information sheet that is provided for participants. This can be requested from the author for those who are interested to know more.

Tip 4: Keeping outsider witnesses on track

Even a well-prepared outsider witness can be tempted to slip into advice-giving or personal story-sharing. Although well-meaning in such digressions, the facilitator should be proactive in bringing the outsider witness's conversations back so they centre on the person they are listening to. It can also be very tempting for the outsider witness to join with the person during their reflections following the outsider witness's contributions, in order to clarify or expand on their previous comments. The role here for the facilitator is to remind participants of the format of the session in which, at this part, the person at the centre of the conversation should be allowed to talk freely without interruption.

Tip 5: Debriefing

The service user is invited to reflect on how they have experienced the session, within the session. The outsider witness is invited to stay on after the session to consider their experience. It is possible that they may have been distressed by what they have heard, so this enables me to check this out and offer support as appropriate. On occasion, a further check-in is offered a day or two later.

A different way of working with ex-service users: letter-writing

Another way in which people can connect and contribute to the lives of others is through the sharing of letters. In my work, I have approached ex-service users to write to current service users, and sometimes there has been some back-and-forth between letter writers.

In writing to the service user, the ex-service user is serving as an audience to the person's stories – their struggles and their responses. This audience position is similar to the outsider witness role outlined above in definitional ceremonies. For the service user who receives a letter that has been written specifically for them, it is likely to result in further reflection on their experiences. Problem-saturated stories of the person's life may have been questioned, leading to opportunities for new understandings of their struggles and their responses. People may find that letters boost their determination to challenge the status quo and see new possibilities for their lives.

The process of letter-writing between people can create connection in their struggles and responses and lessen feelings of difference and isolation. Hope can be passed around through hearing others' stories of courage and of the skills and know-how that has been developed through grapples with adversity. These benefits are not just reserved for the service user, however. The letter writer is likely to engage in a process of reflection of their own journey through difficult times, reminding them of skills and knowledge they developed. This process functions to strengthen their preferred identity and ways of living, enhanced by the service user having been in an audience position for them. Thus, the letter-writing process becomes a mutually beneficial activity.

Experiences of sharing letters

Letters were shared between current service user Robert and ex-service user Paul. Robert spoke of feeling very isolated in the ways he had lived his life. Robert expressed a wish to connect with other men of his age who had experienced something similar to his experiences. I suggested that I ask a man who I had recently worked with, and who had dealt with some similar difficulties, to connect with him via letter-writing. Robert was keen, and so I discussed this with Paul, now an ex-service user. Paul was interested in this initiative. I talked with Robert about what he wanted to share with Paul about himself and the difficulties he was encountering. I then spoke again with Paul, and Paul soon responded with a letter for Robert. Several letters went back and forth between Paul and Robert, facilitated by me, over a couple of months.

On reflecting on this process, Robert said that he was initially surprised that a stranger would do such a positive and kind thing for him. He was not sure what to expect but he found the letters helpful. He spoke of the value of someone having understanding and expressing sympathy towards him, and he valued the sharing of experiences. Robert spoke of how the letters had prompted him to reflect on how people's past had contributed to make them what they are, and how they helped him to think about who he was.

Paul told me that when he was asked to write a letter to a fellow patient, he was immediately keen, but with some concern about his potential forthrightness. Although Robert's and Paul's lives had been lived in quite different ways, Paul did find that he could easily identify with Robert. He expressed hope that their very different approaches to very similar problems would offer an alternative, positive strategy which could be helpful. He hoped that his empathy could inspire Robert to view his situation differently and that this could cause him to review his attitudes.

Paul further reflected that in helping another person, he had felt useful, saying, 'The prospect of my experiences to be a helpful torch made me feel relevant and valued'. Paul also shared the positive effects for him, saying that 'Writing the letter did confirm to me that I had used good ways to deal with my own situation'. It affirmed for him how he had dealt with difficult times and the choices he had made in how he had lived his life. Paul described the letter-writing exercise as a 'real delight' and expressed, 'I can honestly say that I have no regrets'.

To conclude: personal reflections on collaborating with ex-service users as part of therapy

For me, these practices of working alongside ex-service users provide an antidote to any sense of personal helplessness. It is very rewarding to witness how this style of involvement is of assistance to current service users and to those who are no longer accessing the service. The connection and resonance created among people offers authentication, solidarity and hope. I am frequently struck by the extent of these effects, and in awe of the power brought about by the connection and the resonance in the room. This seems to reach far beyond something which I, as an individual therapist, can offer. The impacts that these practices have for participants are positive, considerable and immediate. I would absolutely recommend that therapists consider incorporating these ways of working.

> **INVITATION TO REFLECT**
>
> - What do you think it would be like to take part in a definitional ceremony?
> - Are you surprised to read how moving this can be for both the person at the centre and the outsider witness?
> - What do you think about the idea of bringing together service users in this way?

As discussed, I worked with a service-user engagement group to develop information sheets for people invited to participate in definitional ceremonies. I am happy to share these if they can be helpful and can be contacted at helencarter@nhs.net.

Recommended reading

Denborough, D. (2008) *Collective Narrative Practice*. Adelaide: Dulwich Centre Publications.

White, M. and Epston, D. (1990) *Narrative Means to Therapeutic Ends*. New York: W.W. Norton.

CHAPTER 8

Out of Therapy and into Life

WORKING WITH GROUPS AND COMMUNITIES

Elizabeth Field, Liz Jennings and Chris Norris
with contributions from Polly Kaiser and Asesha Morjaria-Keval

So far in this book, much of what we have discussed has taken place with individuals in healthcare settings such as the NHS. In this chapter, we would like to share with you what we have discovered as we have taken narrative therapy practices into groups and then out of healthcare and into community settings.

This type of work is called 'collective narrative practice', and different methodologies have been developed around the world to support communities to address the hardships and traumas they have faced (Denborough 2008). We thought some of these practices would have relevance to our work with older people and those living with dementia who live in a practically and emotionally challenging world of stigma, with social discourses of decline, disability and disconnection (Offord and Field 2013). This chapter will share practical examples of how we, Elizabeth, Polly and Asesha (clinical psychologists), Liz (a writer and group facilitator) and Keith and Chris (people living with dementia) have used narrative practices with groups and communities to challenge stigma, raise awareness, thicken preferred stories and build connection and solidarity. As several of us have contributed sections, we have put our names as a heading, so you know who is writing.

As in previous chapters, where text appears in boxes, this is our attempt to explain techniques or theory; if these are of less interest, they can be passed over to keep the continuity of the story.

Narrative practices in post-diagnostic courses for those newly diagnosed with dementia
Elizabeth

When we first set out to develop post-diagnostic courses for people newly diagnosed with dementia, I was drawn to narrative practices that challenge stigma and promote the linking of lives. We encouraged conversations that externalised the difficulties dementia brings, such as isolation, and focused on strengthening preferred stories of roles, interests and values that continued. We made sure people were able to bring any friends and family they wanted to, involved people with lived experience in talking to the group, and ended with a shared meal or walk to promote connection after the course ended.

The more we talked with people with dementia, the more we all realised there was much to be done to challenge the stigma and social discourses of decline and disconnection. Keith, Asesha, other colleagues and I started forming dementia engagement groups (Oliver, Stembridge and Lugg 2022) and linking up with other groups nationally through DEEP, the Dementia Engagement and Empowerment Project (www.dementiavoices.org.uk). As Denborough (2008) describes, the experience of making a contribution to the lives of others can often help in reducing or changing the nature of the difficulties and sparking possibilities that ripple through life. This has certainly been our experience as we have worked together alongside people living with dementia and allies.

Tree of Life

One of the narrative practices we have found most useful in our community work with people living with dementia has been the Tree of Life (Denborough 2014; Ncube 2006, 2017; Ncube and Denborough 2007). The Tree of Life is a narrative practice, which uses the metaphor of a tree for a person's life, to help people tell their preferred stories in ways that make them stronger. Liz and Elizabeth have used this in care homes, community groups and with mixed ages at a retreat centre, but Elizabeth started with some willing dementia activists from a few of the DEEP groups (Field 2017; Sinden, Field and Elias 2018). Chris Norris, who lives with dementia, takes up our story, with the help of Keith and

Annemarie, who were also participants living with dementia. For those who would like to understand more about the detail of running a Tree of Life workshop, please see the box below.

> **TREE OF LIFE**
>
> Tree of Life facilitation uses many narrative therapy techniques, including scaffolding, externalising, re-authoring and re-membering, to help people tell detailed preferred stories of competency, possibility, resilience and courage. These are stories that account for the complexity of life and enhance possibilities for relationships or future actions.
>
> **Part 1 – Drawing the tree:** Facilitators use questions to help people identify and thicken alternative stories of strengths, skills and hopes. These are written and drawn onto paper trees. Group members are encouraged to spot abilities, dreams and values in others as they listen to each other's stories.
>
> **Part 2 – The forest of life:** The trees are put up together to create a forest. Using outsider witness questions, participants' preferred stories are thickened as people offer a response to each other's stories and share what they noticed and connected to. This linking of lives develops individual stories into a community story.
>
> **Part 3 – Storms, effects and responses:** Problems are not looked at until after people have been able to tell and hear their identity, no longer dominated by the problem. Then the problems faced are considered as 'storms', along with their effects, their responses to them and the resources available to manage them. This encourages a collaborative approach to problem-solving (Ncube 2017).
>
> **Part 4 – Celebration:** This is a celebration with food, music, fun and a ceremony of certificate-giving. These are personalised to highlight skills, knowledge, hopes and dreams and provide

> further opportunities to enrich preferred stories. Witnesses can be invited to this.

Part 1: Drawing the tree
Chris

I am a member of the East Kent Forget Me Nots group, made up of people living with dementia, NHS professionals, students and volunteers. We support each other around the challenges of living with dementia while educating society at large as to the best ways to facilitate, work with and enable those who have the condition, through ongoing engagement and inclusion. At one of our meetings, Elizabeth shared with us her learning about a counselling therapy method called the Tree of Life that has been used to assist people who are affected by either medical or family problems, and which is a process to calm those traumatised by the effects of life. We were keen to trial this with a group of people living with dementia to establish what benefits we might gain to enhance our lives.

The day of the workshop arrived, and I attended with a degree of trepidation. Previously, I had been involved in therapy sessions where I had looked at my life in detail, and I had not really enjoyed the experience. I had come to the conclusion that some things are best left locked away in the brain for good reason. I was prepared to give it a good go, thinking nothing ventured, nothing gained. However, by the end of the session, I realised I had thoroughly enjoyed myself.

We arrived at our normal meeting hall to find the tables laid out with colouring pens, pencils and copious amounts of fruit- and flower-shaped Post-it notes. This was obviously going to be a hands-on session of doing and not just talking. Elizabeth then explained to us the origins of the Tree of Life and how we were all going to draw our own tree. The roots, ground, trunk, branches, leaves, fruit and seeds all represented symbolic parts of what makes us as a person, aspects of our life and what we would like to leave behind for future generations. The first moment of apprehension struck me as I am not very good at drawing, and I feared my tree would look like it had been struck by Dutch elm disease or ravaged by a forest fire! Thankfully, we were each provided with a printed bare skeleton of a tree to draw and work on, which I guess you could say I found to be a TREEmendous relief! The work, fun and laughter now began. Each element of the make-up of the tree was split into mini-sessions with us filling in the relevant information and comments after a short talk as to what was applicable to that section.

TOP TIPS TO GET OFF TO A GOOD START WITH THE TREE OF LIFE

- Start with an icebreaker to help people feel comfortable with each other.
- Share the southern African background where the Tree of Life was developed. This helps people to understand the context of what they are about to undertake, and it also feels important in offering credit to those who have developed a tool that we find so valuable.
- Facilitators use their trees to introduce themselves and interview each other about them. This demonstrates what is involved and shows the links between the different elements and how we all have multiple stories.
- Ensure people know they need only share what they want to.
- Have pre-drawn templates of trees, leaves, flowers and fruit for people to use if they want to. As one participant said, 'I really liked the templates – it took some pressure off the early decision-making and helped with the uncertainty that people feel at the beginning of a group'.
- Use large visual prompts to remind people which elements of the tree represent which aspects of their lives, and in Part 3 to highlight storms and responses.
- Start anywhere on the tree. The ground can give people something tangible and familiar to focus on which can help with getting going. Leaves enable people to stop thinking about

- themselves for a few minutes, and that often unsticks them. Weave between the different parts with your questions.
- For the roots, invite conversations about music, nature, favourite places, foods, traditions, sayings, faith and special people who have taught them skills and more. It's not about their difficult childhood but what nourishes and supports.
- Double listening is important; attending to stories of survival and resistance as people tell their stories of trauma, vulnerability and injustice means they are less likely to be re-traumatised (White 2004b).
- Listening out for the absent but implicit can be a rich source of skills, knowledges and values.
- Take it slowly to avoid outpacing some participants. Allow enough time for each part of the process.
- Some people found photos of important people or other items helped spark memories.
- Encourage people to be as creative or straightforward as they would like. There is no right way to represent the tree.
- Create prompt sheets for facilitator questions to help everyone stick to narrative questions.
- In Part 2, spend time dwelling on the metaphor of a forest and considering its beauty, and how the trees survive the storms, disease and attack. Then consider their own life storms and responses.
- Consider whether to do it in a day or over several sessions, in person or online. (Field 2017; Sinden et al. 2018; D. Gaynor, personal communication, July 2024)

Chris

I will now explain some of the things that were recorded on my tree to give you an example.

Roots – personal background/what sustains you

My family consisted of my father, mother and five siblings. I guess I was the rebel as all the other five went to university, but I went to the University of Life by joining the army as a musician at 15 years old. Being in the forces from such a young age changed my life completely by instilling a strong sense of self-discipline and strength of character in me that has stood me well throughout my life.

Ground – present life and what you do

The main thing that has been carried through from my roots is my love of music. I still play my tenor horn in brass bands and on bandstands around Kent and beyond.

Trunk – strengths, skills and abilities

There were many things recorded on the trunk, among which were: my ability to see the positive in a negative; my children have turned out well; my sense of humour. Although when people say I'm funny, I can't be sure they mean it in a comical way!

Branches – hopes, goals, wishes and dreams

These are to continue to live my life to the full in spite of dementia, and to inspire others living with dementia so that they can carry on achieving things in life following a diagnosis.

Leaves – important people in your life

Here, of course, were recorded family members and close friends.

Fruits and flowers – gifts given and received, respectively

Support, belief, understanding. Inspiration, friendship, confidence.

Seeds – the legacy you want to leave

Greater understanding around dementia. Initially, I found some elements difficult to do, as it is hard to record what you think other people see as your good aspects, but, by doing so, it helps you to dwell on and acknowledge the positive features of who you are.

Elizabeth

Without input, people can rush ahead writing and talking about difficult experiences in ways that upset them. This is where curious questions and double listening for alternative or implicit stories is crucial. One participant described how this process helped her reassess her parents' care of her, seeing what they had done, not just the care that had been missing. She shared her tree and her new knowledge with them, and they were able to improve their relationship going forward, with a new preferred story with new actions.

Part 2: The forest of life

FIGURE 8.1 THE FOREST
(Sinden et al. 2018)

Chris

The individual trees were mounted beside each other on the wall to form a forest of trees. We all wandered around the room looking at each tree, armed with the fruit and flower-shaped Post-it notes. As we read each tree, we wrote messages on notes about the gifts of fruits and flowers that the person had given us. These were not material gifts but gifts of being cared about, acts of kindness, friendship, inspiration, confidence, etc. When we had finished this, we all then examined our own tree and were able to see how much we were appreciated by the others in the group.

Elizabeth

While listening to people telling their stories, participants were encouraged to identify skills held by others and discuss any gifts others in the group may have given them. For me, the chance to witness how stories strengthened people and built connections was truly moving. Chris and David learned of their mutual love of music and decided to perform together for the dementia activists' summer party the following month and at many other events. Keith, a long-standing member of a dementia activists' group, told a newer member that he had been contemplating retiring from that group because of the tensions between people, but had continued because of her enthusiasm for the work. She had been wondering about her contribution's worth and a couple of weeks later commented this about the experience: 'The other thing that remained with me was the generosity and wonderful comments I received from other members of the Forget Me Nots group, some of which brought me to tears. I will always remember the way these comments made me feel on the day'. She became more involved, even chairing meetings for the first time.

Part 3: Storms, effects and responses

This is the time to acknowledge the difficulties people face. In dementia groups, people mostly talk about the impact of stigma. Stories were shared of arms being stroked, pitying looks and assumptions they could not go out alone or were dangerous to others. As mood and memory are linked, and dementia can make emotional regulation more difficult, participants found it best to consider storms and responses at the same time. As Annemarie put it, 'Thinking about all the storms is a bit depressing…by the time you get to the sunshine, you've already gone there [the storms] and you're already in that negative mindset so it's harder to think of the sunshine…better to alternate between a storm and a positive…'

For responses to storms, participants told stories of still going out alone, trying new things, making new relationships and speaking out publicly on social media, to the press and in training events. People agreed that to live well with dementia you need to be a bendy willow tree rather than an oak. 'Flexibility', 'strength', 'resilience' and 'adaptability' were words often used, along with 'tenacity' to help them stand their ground and 'Teflon' to let things slide off.

FIGURE 8.2 STORMS, EFFECTS AND RESPONSES
(Sinden et al. 2018)

Part 4: Celebration

This involves a party. We have usually gone for tea, cake, music and a ceremony of certificate-giving. The certificates record some of the skills and knowledge of the person, and some of their hopes and dreams. Where possible, including family and friends provides opportunities to continue enriching preferred stories using outsider witness practices (Ncube 2017). Participants take home both their tree and certificate to support retelling their friends and family about the day and what was meaningful to them. 'My tree is on my study door, so I see it every day, and if I am feeling a bit low, I look at it and it makes me feel heaps better. I think everyone should do the workshop as a boost to their self-esteem'.

Reflections on the Tree of Life
Chris

So, is there value in doing a Tree of Life session? The answer is a resounding *yes*. I found that it takes you back in a positive way to make you realise what makes you the person that you are. It helps you focus on your strengths. So often after a diagnosis of dementia, you can feel that you no longer have a value, but this therapy helps to restore your self-esteem. Getting a dementia diagnosis can be like a tree losing all its leaves in winter. However, with the right nourishment and support, it can spring back just as strong but with new growth.

A constant throughout the day was the laughter and humorous stories that we told each other around events that had happened in our lives. It was very uplifting and encouraging to hear others describe your attributes and to read the positive comments on each of our trees. It is good to hear how you have had a positive effect in their lives. I totally recommend doing a therapy session like this in a group as it moves things away from the clinical one-to-one setting. Without doubt, being part of a Tree of Life group session helps you, as the song says, to 'Always Look on the Bright Side of Life' and to realise the true value that you have in your life both personally and for those people you come into contact with. You see that you haven't lost everything after a dementia diagnosis. It helps you acknowledge that there is so much more to you than you realise and plenty more that you can still achieve in life. I think it's the best type of therapy I have ever done. Normally, when we do therapy, we talk about all the bad things, but here we were talking about the positives and the wonderful things in our lives rather than the things that drag us down with dementia and the challenges around our family.

Elizabeth

I was surprised by how many, and how much, people with dementia appreciated doing the Tree of Life. To quote Annemarie again, 'If I could only do one thing before I die it would be the Tree of Life'.

I think some of the reasons why the Tree of Life has been so popular with people with dementia is because it enables people to experience competence in things that matter to them: connecting with their roots, with others and with future hopes and dreams. In fact, as a narrative practice, the Tree of Life has many benefits for people with cognitive difficulties. The onus is on the therapist to scaffold questions in such a way that the person is able to answer them, moving in gradual steps from the known and familiar to the possible to know. Memories are sought by theme or traits with no need for chronological order. The metaphor of the different parts of the tree breaks the task down into manageable sections, and prompts reduce the need to remember what the Tree of Life is. It is able to accommodate both common experiences and allow space for the particular. We had been worried that some people with dementia would struggle with the metaphor or that doing a task that required memory, language, writing and turn-taking might highlight disabilities; that was not the case. Many reported becoming more aware of their hopes and goals and experienced a sense of competence and community with others and a lifting in mood that lasted. As one participant put it:

> Our Tree of Life…was an excellent way to keep us focusing and sharing our broken minds…I liked so much the Tree of Life workshop because for me, living with dementia, it is very important to socialise, and we did that in a very warm ambience. Dementia breaks our short memory and spoils our ability to concentrate, making us anxious. On that day, by taking us back in our lives, we were able to concentrate on the past and feel relaxed while putting our lives like some lovely trees with roots, trunk and branches with green foliage. A very positive result. Let's do more workshops like this!

Chris, Keith and others went on to share their experiences in workshops for staff, students and the 3 Nations Dementia Working Group (3NDWG), challenging the discourses they identified as storms and thickening their preferred stories of 'people who can'.

Adaptations of the Tree of Life in creative writing groups for people with dementia
Liz
Recently, I was in a group talking with eight older people about some of the things they enjoyed. Someone spoke of their love of music, and

immediately seven voices chimed in with, 'I'm not musical!', 'I'm hopeless!', 'I wish I was musical!' Finally, one chap said, 'I was told by my teacher when I was 7 years old that on a scale of 1 to 10, my voice was a minus 5 and I haven't sung since, not even in the shower'.

I think a lot of what drives me in my work facilitating creative groups is the desire to give people a chance to tell new stories about who they are, and to delight in diminishing those negative voices.

When Elizabeth introduced me to the Tree of Life, I felt so excited by the ways this tool could enable people to do this. I've found that it's a very flexible tool that can be fruitfully adapted for all sorts of settings. I've used it with groups like the Forget Me Nots as a way of reflecting on their group's identity. Used in this way, the leaves become all the group members and those involved in making the group happen, from the venue hosts to those who approve the budget for this group to continue. The leaves become a place of realising that this group exists because of a large family of supporters and advocates – an encouraging thought.

I've used the Tree of Life as an evaluation tool, enabling groups to build up a visual picture to review a project. We filled the trunk with all the new skills people had gained through the project, and the branches with the things that people hoped to explore and develop now that the project itself was coming to an end. This was really powerful because often after groups that have been terrific fun, participants can feel quite flat. By using the branches of the tree, people thought through the next steps for themselves and chose ways forward that excited them personally.

Often in workshops, someone will say, 'Trees are the lungs of the planet', and this image is entirely appropriate, because what I have seen the Tree of Life do is give people a chance to *breathe*. In pausing to reflect and then to share and thicken our stories, and to forge new connections through those stories, we seem to inhale and then exhale as one. There's a collective sigh of relief at the realisation that we are not alone; we stand as a forest, and we are all connected both through our pasts and through our futures as we share and encourage one another in building towards our hopes and dreams.

At the end of each year, I often find myself involved in festive events and celebrations across a variety of groups. I'm always on the lookout for fresh ideas for these times together, and the opportunity to adapt the Tree of Life for Christmas was too good to pass up! (See the box below.) Towards the end of each year, many dictionaries announce their 'word of the year'. I encourage each person to choose a word of their own to declare over their life for the year to come. Choosing this word can be a significant act for people as, essentially, they focus in on a vision statement in a single word. In the most recent group I ran, one man chose the word 'forgiveness' and spoke about how he wanted to set some relationships right in the next year. Another woman chose 'creativity' and spoke about having realised in the thinking process that she wanted to make a point of enjoying art more in the way she used to and had let go of in recent years. People start to talk about the things they're looking forward to, which can be really helpful, especially if they have had a tough year.

FIGURE 8.3 A CHRISTMAS TREE OF LIFE

> **CHRISTMAS TREE OF LIFE**
>
> We start with an outline of a Christmas tree with some presents at the bottom.
>
> - *The pot*: Write on the pot some of the things that have kept you 'rooted' this year – the solid support that you rely on and value.
> - *Strings of lights*: Each light represents a person, living or dead, who lights up your life. Write their name or initials onto each light.
> - *Baubles*: Add these and fill each one with something you do that brings you joy. Take a moment to hold a bauble and enjoy the beauty of it – they really are joyful objects, a burst of colour and reflected light.
> - *Gifts under the tree*: These are wrapped and as yet unknown. In these, write your hopes, dreams or prayers for the year to come.
> - *Star on the top* (declaring a new storyline for your identity): Finally, draw a large star at the top of the tree and choose your word for the year.

Elizabeth

The Tree of Life is endlessly adaptable in mental health contexts as well. Asesha and I have created the trees on inpatient wards (Field 2017; Fraser et al. 2018). In community mental health settings, Danielle runs Tree of Life workshops over two half-days (D. Gaynor, personal communication, July 2024), and Dan ran a 12-session group (Blake and Kaiser 2019). Polly found Tree of Life helpful in exploring values and hopes for dementia-friendly Black majority churches and that it resonated with the biblical background of many of the African/Caribbean participants. In all these contexts, the Tree of Life has proved helpful in creating connection and community.

As discussed in the opening chapter, many of us have been drawn to a narrative approach, as it works against an 'expert' position and enables us to feel we truly collaborate, as fellow human beings, with the people we work with. It is not surprising then that doing this work also moves us. Sharon, who was helping to facilitate the Tree of Life group with Dan, went home and, never having written a poem in her life, wrote this:

> *What grounds me is what surrounds me.*
> *It's a mixture of things past and the now*
> *It makes things happen somehow.*
> *It's the ground that feeds the very roots*
> *That gives life to new buds, leaves and shoots.*
> *Who knows which way they will grow?*
> *They all owe their thanks to the ground below.*
> *That ground may be rich, earthy and nourishing,*
> *Or light, sandy and perpetually shifting.*
> *Whichever way the land lies for you*
> *Stand tall, look around and admire the view.*
> *Take a moment to appreciate what you have now,*
> *'Cos that moment will pass, before you know how.*
> *Precious moments support and surround us,*
> *They keep us who we are, they ground us.*

SHARON BARROW (MAY 2018, WITH KIND PERMISSION)

Evaluation of the Tree of Life

Most of the situations where we have used the Tree of Life have been funded by organisations and not by the participants themselves, and so there is a need for demonstrating impact. As you have seen above, the richest source has been discussions with the participants themselves and the examples they have highlighted about how their lives have changed. However, sometimes there are requests for other forms of feedback. We have found the Canterbury Wellbeing Scale (Johnson et al. 2015) useful for evaluating dementia groups. Danielle Gaynor (personal communication, July 2024) developed a questionnaire to try and capture change in her use of the Tree of Life in mental health settings, which she kindly shares in the box below.

> Rate each question on this scale: not at all/a little/somewhat/quite a bit/very much.
>
> - I can see strengths in myself.
> - I know what is important to me in life.
> - There are things in my life that I am proud of.
> - I feel able to cope with life's challenges.
> - I have hopes and plans.

Using poetry and outsider witness practices to strengthen connections and document experience

Outsider witness practices, as we saw in Chapter 7, can have a powerful positive impact on people's lives. Asesha and colleagues used outsider witness practices to ask people, newly diagnosed with dementia attending post-diagnostic courses, to respond to writings by others with dementia and carers. People's responses were written down, which the facilitators pulled together into poetry or prose. The writings co-created with the first group were shared to inspire the second group, whose writings were shared with the third group and so on. The collective documents were also shared with family and friends and put publicly on display. In this way, the writings and the collective witnessing of the writings linked the lives of these individuals and groups, thus broadening and expanding a shared connectedness and bringing together communities of support for those living alongside dementia (Morjaria-Keval 2024). As her participants described it:

> 'It's really quite moving to hear other people's experiences from the last group. It makes me feel like I'm not alone with this and that it's ok to have the feelings I have' (Joan, living with dementia).

'It's powerful. Those writings hit the nail on the head... It's almost like they are describing myself' (Simone, carer).

'When you can't find an answer or make sense of it as an individual, it helps knowing what others' circumstances are...and how they are dealing with it' (John, carer). (Morjaria-Keval 2024, p.37)

Polly has also worked with poetry and outsider witness practices to strengthen connections and to allow people to give voice to their experience.

Polly

Greater Manchester Mature Minds Matters was established with older people with 'lived experience' of mental health issues. Their creative project 'Rhymes from the Wise' enabled older people to come together and talk about issues which affect them in a safe, non-judgemental, creative space. We hoped that this would help challenge the discourses that it's 'normal' to be 'depressed when you are old' and enable people to access support. Four workshops were held across Greater Manchester facilitated by local poet J Ahmed and me. Everyone spoke and everyone, miraculously, wrote poems. Drawing on the idea that 'narrative practice is founded on the idea that the stories that we tell about ourselves are not private and individual but are a social achievement' (Fox, Tench and Marie 2002), we used outsider witness practices to explore the impact of the poetry project and its effects on participants' lives and their identities.

I interviewed two members of the group, James and Freddi, while Val, Deanne and Kate, who had also taken part, acted as witnesses to the conversation. We heard about some of the difficulties that people had experienced in life: bullying, harassment, racism, parental and spousal mental ill health, physical health challenges and being carers. Group members belong to different religious, cultural and socio-economic groups, with some members from the LGBT community. This way of working enabled people to share their commonalities as older people with lived experience of mental health challenges, and all spoke with passion about the impact of the poetry project on their lives. As explained by Deanne, 'It struck me – what we have in common. We need to express ourselves in poetry. We can speak about things we are not brave enough to speak about. I do journalling and it's my "poetic processing" getting it out of our heads and onto paper, sharing it. There's a necessity to voice'.

Why poetry?

I began by asking 'why poetry?' and learned what it meant to Freddi to be able to be creative, when her experience was having this 'knocked out of you at a very early age'. It was moving to hear her say, 'I felt I'd come home' and to hear James say, 'it feeds your heart and spirit'. I learned from them both that 'poetry is a way of saying stuff that you can't say to anyone else ever' (Freddi). James added, 'It's part of what maintains good mental health…men don't talk about their emotions that much – but they can through poetry'.

I also learned about the value in hearing from one another: 'Witnessing and being witnessed, hearing other people's stories and how they overcame struggles… Well, I was impressed by how people just keep going' (James), and the importance of 'keeping vitality alive', which James explained gets harder with age.

Fighting stigma

One of the important themes that emerged was that of fighting stigma and 'doing justice', which both Freddi and James emphasised. They shared their views about the difficulties of a medicalising view of mental health and the way in which older people are told 'it's just part of being old' (Freddi). The poetry project stood in contrast to this, as James explains: 'We pathologise mental health, and standing in someone else's shoes is vital. Poetry helps people stand in someone else's shoes – hopefully, it will help people understand older people's mental health and help to reduce stigma too'.

Val, Deanne and Kate as outsider witnesses resonated with these themes. We heard how their different faith traditions helped them in doing justice and sustained their passion for change and justice. Both

Deanne and Kate illustrated for us how the societal stigma they grew up with around mental health caused damage that they have now been able to address. 'We carry the scars so it's good to talk – it's important to share stories...a lot of us are carrying wounds from childhood...we couldn't talk about mental health back then' (Deanne).

Legacy and action

For Freddi, her commitment is to write more poems, speaking them out loud and having them published: 'Books! More books!' She would also like to see facilities in the community where people, young and old, can come together to write and share. James spoke about how he had taken part in a project about end-of-life care at the Manchester LGBT Foundation where they had created a memory box. He said his poem would be put in his box and be said at his funeral.

For Val, discovering how poetry could help her when she lay in bed, physically ill with few outlets, was vitally important. She spoke about the importance of paying attention to the link between physical health and mental health. She now helps others and is a keen poetry champion.

Deanne and Kate shared advice that they would like to share with you here. From Deanne: 'My grandmother always said, "You must be the best version that you can be." That always made me determined. You hit a certain age, and you are invisible. This is different in different cultures. It used to be that you respected the elders. People need to be listened to'.

And from Kate: 'My advice and action is vitality, walking the walk, keeping active and keeping engaged. Art therapy comes in many different forms – it's not a one-size-fits-everybody'.

Other creative ways to support preferred identities and preferred stories
Liz

Like the members of Mature Minds Matter, Keith, Chris and I have used arts projects to challenge the stigma and create alternative stories of all that people with dementia can do. This started with a life-writing class that resulted in a book, *Welcome to Our World* (Jennings 2014), the first book in the world by a group of people with dementia. Then we ran the Dementia Friendly Film Club, setting out to blast through the then prevalent assumption that dementia cinema equalled *Singing in the Rain* and *The Sound of Music* on a loop. This was a discourse that was so limiting! We created a space where people with dementia could enjoy modern films and then discuss the themes and plots in a sociable atmosphere. We were invited to the British Film Institute to speak to a group of cinema owners about the experiences of our group. It was a thrilling opportunity to challenge people's preconceived assumptions about the story of dementia with exciting real-life results: the film our large group had most enjoyed was a subtitled Chinese film with a very complex storyline dealing with gritty issues. About as far from *Singing in the Rain* as you could get!

This was followed by a number of exciting creative projects, such as people with dementia writing film scripts which were performed locally, an online poetry class which led to the publication of *Time and Place* (Jennings 2020) and a photography project where people created books of their preferred stories of identity through photos and poems. Chris and the Ashford Phoenix dementia engagement group challenged the idea that people with dementia cannot learn new things when they learned to play the ukulele and compose music together.

Most recently, we have worked with Jasper Bouverie of Funder Films CIC on 'Pix to Flix', a project enabling participants to tell a preferred story of their choosing about themselves using their own photographs. Dawn's story is particularly powerful. She tells the story of her daughter, who was murdered by her partner. Dawn was resolute in her desire to share this: she wanted people to know that the worst had happened, and she had survived. Moreover, she had reinvented herself and found a new way to live. Now, diagnosed with dementia, she is reinventing herself once again. Reflecting on the experience, she explained how making the film had given her closure: 'These projects do change you and they do help'. She has since published *Dawn's Dementia Field Guide* to help others diagnosed with dementia (Horne 2024).

There are many more examples of how people living with dementia or older people have challenged the discourses that seek to limit them, by living their lives, sharing their wisdom and creating art to enrich us all. We have listed some of these below and would love to hear those you know about.

So, as we finish the chapter, we hope we have given you a sense of the power of collective narrative practices in addressing the impact of negative discourses and problematic stories of dementia, mental illness or ageing. We hope you have caught some of the fun and playfulness that can be healing. Finally, we hope we have sparked your creativity to go and try new things in new places.

> **INVITATION TO REFLECT**
>
> - Who or which ideas have inspired you?
> - How would you like to use collective narrative practices to support communities you are part of?
> - Who might you link with?

Useful resources

www.dementiavoices.org.uk for more about the Dementia Engagement and Empowerment Project (DEEP).

www.dementiaenquirers.org.uk for research and investigations by people living with dementia and the outcome of Ashford Phoenix's ukulele project.

www.kmpt.nhs.uk/get-involved/participation-and-involvement/living-with-dementia/forget-me-nots for links to projects such as Pix to Flix, Telling Your Friends and Family, and Time and Place.

https://brightshadow.org.uk – arts projects for people with dementia.

www.youtube.com/channel/UCvu7LgCL6G1n0DA6iGoBraw – the Pix to Flix films by Dawn, Keith and others can be watched here.

www.gmopn.org.uk/rhymesfromthewise for the poems from Mature Minds Matter.

https://dulwichcentre.com.au for projects, songs and resources in other languages.

https://phola.org for more of Ncube's work.

CHAPTER 9

Supporting Colleagues

HOLDING ONTO HOPE AND CONNECTION

Gemma Barry and Elizabeth Field
with contributions from Jane Grant, Polly Kaiser,
Asesha Morjaria-Keval, Rosslyn Offord and Becky Scullion

As you have read in earlier chapters, many of us were initially drawn to narrative practices for our clinical work. We soon realised that they had something nourishing to offer us and our colleagues also. This is what we wish to share with you in this chapter.

In the NHS, where many of us work, staff are under ever-increasing levels of stress, morale is low and people talk of feeling burnt out. Studies to explore and understand the challenges of burnout in nurses found that negative relationships, poor supervision, poor leadership, negative team relationships and high psychological demands were commonly cited as contributory (Dall'Ora et al. 2020). Others have found that poor well-being at work can relate to feeling that your views aren't valued by higher management (Ravalier, McVicar and Boichat 2020). Reynolds (2011a) writes that burnout occurs in response to social injustice. She says that harm comes from witnessing the injustices people experience and the frustration we have at being powerless to change or influence these societal structures. We have learned from her that trying to cure burnout with self-care and an emphasis on resilience risks blaming individual staff and diverting attention from the unjust contexts that have led to the colleague's experience of distress.

In this chapter, we will give examples of how narrative maps, outsider witness practices, collective documents and the Tree of Life can help team members connect with each other, communicate with their management and remain close to their values and strengths. The work we describe has come about at our suggestion or in response to requests for case discussions, staff reflective practice sessions, supervision, workshops, training and supporting communication between clinicians and senior management. We hope that this chapter gives you an insight into how narrative practices, with their focus on values and preferred identities, work so well in the context of a challenging work environment. We hope that it may give you a few ideas to try out.

Many of the practices we discuss here have been introduced earlier in the book; where that is the case, we will let you know where to find out more. For other ideas, there is more detail in boxes. Many people have contributed to this chapter, and at points we will hand over to them to share their work.

Case discussion/formulation

There are differing views within narrative therapy as to the role of formulation, with some seeing it as important and others less so (Meehan and Guilfoyle 2015). Essentially, it is a tool that can help make sense of someone's experiences in their contexts and is a familiar way of working for many professions in the NHS. Polly and Dan describe a practice they introduced with staff, using narrative ideas to support the development of new skills and ways of thinking about the clients they are working with.

Polly

A conversation Dan and I had with key stakeholders in a day hospital highlighted the hope to develop skills in psychological formulation. We chose to introduce the team to a narrative approach to formulation as this would align with the team's values, while also having the potential to stimulate new ways of working and 'thicken' or augment the team's strengths in delivering person-centred care. It involved asking the team what they knew about the clients' problems, relationships and strengths, then recording their answers on a flipchart (see the box below). A form was developed so that a record was available in the notes after each session (Figure 9.1). This was trialled in morning handovers and became known as doing a 'stickperson' (Blake and Kaiser 2019). A stickperson for a staff member was also developed with clients, so that they were aware of the process taking place in morning handovers.

Questions to explore the problem:

- What keeps the problem(s) alive?
- Who is affected by the problem(s)?

Questions to explore the person and other available stories – their relationships, strengths, skills and abilities:

- If the problem wasn't getting in the way, what would the person be doing?
- What is important to the person?

Questions to collect what we are curious about and ideas for moving forward with this person as a team:

- Would anyone like to have a conversation with the person based on the information we have collected today? What would that conversation be about?

Many rich descriptions came from the outsider witness group we subsequently ran to evaluate this approach. One colleague reflected that these ways of working 'help me to remember what the job is about'. They found this reassuring, as it can be easy to lose sight of this in the context of a busy and demanding work environment. These practices also reconnected us with our own values and opened up new possibilities for our own future practice.

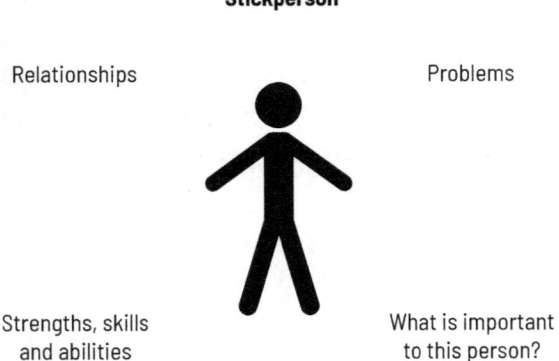

FIGURE 9.1 RECORDING FORM FOR 'STICKPERSON' SESSIONS DEVELOPED BY JADE INNS (*BLAKE AND KAISER* 2019)

Narrative practices to support staff teams

While the above example focused on using narrative techniques to help a staff team understand more about their clients, we also frequently draw on these techniques to support staff themselves. As discussed at the start of this chapter, the NHS can be a challenging context to work in. When we are asked to support staff teams, we want to do this in ways that acknowledge the social injustices staff witness (Reynolds 2011a), which offer support in ways that fit with their values. Narrative therapy techniques can be used to acknowledge the problem stories and develop the preferred stories that make people stronger, as we saw in Polly and Dan's work. These narrative practices can help inspire and invigorate teams by fostering a sense of shared solidarity and connection to both personal and professional skills, knowledge and values.

Narrative maps
Becky

Drawing on narrative practices has been invaluable to me when offering reflective practice spaces to staff teams. I find that Michael White's statement of position maps (White 2007), as explained in Chapter 2, can be a helpful framework to guide such conversations. They invite a style of conversation that enables staff members to notice and name the discourses and 'problem stories' that may be impacting on their everyday working lives and connect to stories of strength, resilience, experience and knowledge that may have become less visible in the face of challenges. Approaching these conversations with an appreciation that there is always more to the 'problem story' being told (White 2007) helps me to invite a conversation about other layers in their story and whether their current relationship with work is or isn't fitting with their hopes/intentions for coming into their profession. Externalising the problem, as explained in Chapter 2, is part of this process, and is illustrated in the following example.

I spoke with a colleague during a reflective practice session who told me about her sense of exhaustion and disappointment about how her role was not 'adding up to' her preconceived hopes. She agreed to share more about how Disappointment had come to be part of her life. She spoke of how 'overflowing' her days were with seeing a 'never-ending' list of clients with complex needs, to whom she couldn't dedicate all her time, instead ending up in the office completing endless 'tickbox' exercises. She spoke of how Disappointment often showed up as she got into bed at the end of a day. I wanted to hear more about her experience of living with this. Asking about the effects of Disappointment showing up at the end of the day resulted in her telling stories of how this led to rumination about whether she had made the right decision in her career and how feelings of anxiety, low mood and tiredness followed. As she spoke, other members of the group nodded along and spoke of similar experiences, resonating with aspects of her experiences.

I shared that I would like to ask a question that may seem strange: 'Is this okay with you, what is unfolding here, with Disappointment showing up every night?' She quickly said that it was not okay. She spoke of the effect Disappointment was having in terms of taking away the moments of 'hope' that showed up in her days, such as connecting with her clients, having meaningful conversations or the 'buzz' that came with finding a way forward in complex situations. This opened up further conversations about her and others' hopes and values that they brought to their work. This led to a sharing of experiences about how they 'keep their hopes alive' and 'notice' those 'sparkling moments' in among the day's busyness. Staff spoke about how they could support one another by asking about a positive experience from their day. The group also reflected on the importance of systemic change, and how teams and supervision needed to prioritise these conversations. Actions were agreed about feeding back these ideas in the next team meeting.

Outsider witnessing

As Reynolds (2011a) reminds us, we are social beings who need to feel connected to others in our values and our actions. Asesha has found that outsider witnessing practices allow for colleagues to be seen and heard by others in a way that is connecting and sustaining. Helen has discussed these practices in detail in Chapter 7, but we include a summary box below as a reminder.

> **OUTSIDER WITNESS QUESTIONS**
>
> - *Identify the expression* – What expression caught your attention? What phrase struck a chord?
> - *Describe the image* – What image did this expression evoke? What did the expression and image make you think about the person's values? hopes? commitments?
> - *Embody the response* – What is it about your own experiences that meant this expression or image captured you?
> - *Acknowledging 'transport'* – Where has this experience moved you to that you might not have got to, had you not witnessed this today?

Asesha

I ran reflective sessions with six to eight team members working on an inpatient mental health ward for older people. I reminded the group of the format at each session and gave handouts with the outsider witness questions on. After a brief check-in, a staff member was invited to talk about any aspect of their work that they felt comfortable sharing, and others volunteered as outsider witnesses. Other team members were always invited to share their reflections towards the end, so that everyone could contribute should they wish to.

In one session, I interviewed Ria, who spoke about her dilemma of going for another job that might offer her a new challenge while her current job offered her comfort and familiarity. Ria was clearly a valued colleague who had worked on the ward for years. She spoke of loving her work and described feeling like 'part of the furniture'. Three outsider witnesses were interviewed and spoke about how Ria's story brought them in touch with their own relationship to the caring role they had chosen; one that, despite being poorly paid, was hugely rewarding. Matt acknowledged how he had changed jobs a lot in the past and finally felt a sense of peace and satisfaction knowing he was doing a worthwhile, caring job in which he felt appreciated. Ria shared that she felt conflicted about leaving her job. Despite it sometimes feeling overwhelming and challenging, the shifts allowed her to better manage her physical health, and several years later she was still working there. Gill also shared being torn at times between thoughts of looking for other jobs and worries that new colleagues and a new manager may not understand the struggles she had with her own mental health.

Ria reflected on her surprise and sense of validation to hear that her colleagues also felt, at times, conflicted about staying in their jobs. She drew on aspects of her work that she really appreciated and her specific skills in caring – for example, being able to share complex information with patients in an easily understandable way. The session helped bring out the different caring skills that team members had and appreciated in one another, despite job roles and pay bands. Outsider witness practices enable the acknowledgement of small acts that can help connect people and teams to the intentions they hold for their work. They can also amplify the values, commitments and ethics that are expressed through these small acts.

Outsider witnessing and collective documents

Since poor well-being at work can relate to feeling that your views aren't valued by higher management (Ravalier et al. 2020), Jane sought to use outsider witnessing and collective documents to support staff in their communication with senior managers.

Jane

We found ourselves, as many teams do, working independently with an ever-increasing workload. My colleagues were feeling the brunt of this and increasingly talked to me about how challenging and frustrating things were feeling. I wished to offer support while maintaining a de-centred stance – to privilege my colleagues' experiences, skills and knowledges when communicating their experiences to those more senior than us who may have the power to influence things.

I began by interviewing my colleagues in small groups to witness what had been challenging for them and what they had done to sustain themselves through these challenging times (their skills, knowledges and values). These interviews were often full of emotion as they witnessed each other's experiences for the first time. I then generated themes from the interviews and created a 'collective document' which held all our experiences. The next step was the retelling of the document; we all gathered, and I read the document out. I had a sense that this was an emotional moment to hear their own words retold and for others to join and hear them. It felt like an acknowledgement of shared difficulties or challenges, a shared commitment and an acknowledgement of shared skills, knowledge and values about sustenance and endurance. Some of the themes that emerged were self-awareness, gratitude, holding onto hope and having a connection to others.

Quotes from the interviews were included in the collective document. For example, Mark said: 'Meeting with other colleagues, whose teams weren't under as much pressure… It gave a stable, safe place to stand so I could think'. Next, I invited an audience to witness our experiences. Two representatives from the trust board agreed to read our document and for me to interview them about their responses using the outsider witness framework.

This interview took place online, and my plan was to gather my colleagues to watch the recording. Unfortunately, technology thwarted this as the recording did not work. However, I was able to share with my colleagues the notes that I had taken during this interview.

Louise's reflections were: 'I think people were emotional when you read it out... There was like a togetherness as a team. It's good to know that others know what we have been going through'.

Using a collective document and outsider witnessing as a response to collective trauma as a team was incredibly useful, and privileged the position of the team. We managed as a team to convey our experiences to others, and it was a connecting experience for us all.

TOP TIPS FOR USING OUTSIDER WITNESS PRACTICES WITH STAFF GROUPS

- Prepare your group for what you are looking for. This can help to avoid becoming problem-solving or praising. Explicitly stating that this is not a problem-solving space may give people permission to listen in a different way. Sharing the questions that you are going to be asking them to respond to (ahead of time and as a printout on the day) may also be useful.
- If you are having multiple sessions, take the time at the beginning of each session to remind the group of the structure and format.
- Have a backup in case something goes wrong with technology. This could be in the form of a note-taker or another way of recording the discussion.
- If using outsider witness practice to facilitate reflective practice, try to agree in advance who might be willing to be 'interviewed' at the next meeting. This can help maximise the time you have and give the staff member time to prepare.

Distinguishing skills and ethics

Although outsider witness practice has a specific structure to it, there are times when we might use the principle of witnessing others' stories in a different way to support staff teams. Asesha gives an example of another way shared ethics and values can be collectively acknowledged through the practices of telling and witnessing (see the box below). She demonstrated this in a workshop she ran for senior leaders, designed to share stories to make visible the skills and knowledges they held in relation to their work.

> **DISTINGUISHING SKILLS AND ETHICS**
> *Adapted from 'Distinguishing Skills and Ethics' – an exercise developed by Maggie Carey and used in the Institute of Narrative Therapy's module 'Using Narrative Therapy in the Process of Supervision'.*
>
> In groups of three, the *first person* shares a story in their work that they are pleased with (e.g. something that focuses on holding a person-centred ethic in their practice/management/leadership). This could be a conversation with a colleague or client, or a group or meeting they've facilitated. It can be a small act that expresses what they give value to.
>
> The *second person* (interviewer) asks questions to help the first person give rich description to the story.
>
> The *third person* listens out for skills, abilities and values which they can jot down on Post-it notes. At the end of the story, the third person reads out what they've written to the first person and either sticks the notes onto a piece of paper or the person, keeping one back that particularly resonates with the note-taker.
>
> The *second* person (interviewer) can then use the outsider witness practice to further thicken and connect preferred stories and shared values.
>
> People are encouraged to reverse roles so that all group members can share a story.

Asesha

The exercise described in the box above seemed to have a profoundly connecting effect. People shared that they 'didn't know [each] other's stories' and it enabled them to get in touch with 'why we do what we do'. They expressed a desire to have more of these kinds of experiences, which they felt could support 'team members to have time to reflect' and help 'keep the person at the heart'. One person warmly described the experience leaving her with a 'warm Ready Brek glow feeling' and another shared that she felt better about herself through having taken part in this exercise.

Tree of Life

Elizabeth, Liz and colleagues introduced the Tree of Life in Chapter 8, which is another helpful narrative practice for building connection and meaningful communication, not only in our community groups but also with staff teams. As explained, this approach uses a metaphor of a tree with its roots, ground, trunk, branches and leaves to prompt people to think about what sustains them, their strengths and abilities, important people and hopes for the future (Ncube 2006, 2017; Ncube and Denborough 2007). People share their stories and support each other in identifying further skills before considering the storms they face together and the ways in which they respond to them.

We will go on to share how we have found the Tree of Life supportive to staff groups and a good option for team awaydays where there is a hope for greater connection (the box below has some ideas for questions). We have done it as originated with individual trees put together as a forest and also adapted it to create team trees where everyone's skills, experiences and values contribute to shared dreams and plans of action. Sometimes, we use just the tree and forest elements as a shorter exercise, as Gemma describes below.

TREE OF LIFE QUESTIONS ABOUT PROFESSIONAL IDENTITY
Adapted from Kis-Sines and Pluznik (2014).

- *Roots of the tree* – your background and experiences
  What brought you to this work? Who inspired you? What experiences meant this type of work is a good fit for you?

- *The ground* – your current situation
  Where do you work? How long have you been with this team? What are some of the values and commitments of the job you do that are most meaningful to you? Why are they meaningful? How does this link in with your hopes for your work?

- *Trunk of the tree* – your skills and knowledge
  What skills and knowledge do you bring to your work in this team? What is the history of them? What do others say they value about you as a colleague? Who first noticed these skills that you have?

- *Branches of the tree* – your hopes for the future
  What do you hope for the future of our team? What direction do you hope we go in? What do you hope for the people you work with?

- *Leaves of the tree* – your supporters
  Who supports you in the work you do? Who are the important people that make your work possible?

- *Fruits* – your gifts given and received
  What have others in the team contributed to your development? What have you contributed to other colleagues' development?

Gemma

Rosslyn and I have used the Tree of Life approach as a way of strengthening a shared identity for our small psychology service in a community memory team. Rosslyn introduced this to share hopes and dreams for the service, which could then assist us in prioritising potential service developments. I interviewed our team (Rosslyn, Jo, Sara and Anna) to explore the effects of this approach on us as a team and as individuals.

A key theme that emerged when talking about the process of constructing our 'professional trees' was the pleasure in hearing stories from others about what had brought them into the profession. Paying attention to the roots of people's trees and noticing commonalities in our backgrounds and family narratives felt particularly valuable. Jo, who was new in the team, commented on how helpful she found it to get to know colleagues and quickly feel part of a team. Anna reflected on having a much stronger sense of who we all were and what values we shared.

Noticing the values we shared, such as fairness, compassion and respecting clients' autonomy, helped us to shape some team values that we hold, which we revisit at times when we have new staff members or difficult decisions to make. In thinking about these values, Jo reflected on feeling that the exercise had a sense of equality about it. She commented that she was mindful that we are all at different 'pay grades' and have different experience but felt that wasn't relevant in terms of people's contributions being prioritised. Sara appreciated the chance to be creative.

We discussed the practicalities of the exercise and recognised that it could not be rushed. It required at least an hour and a half, as it was important to allow sufficient time to construct and share parts of our trees. Anna reflected on us as a group of women with a lot in common and recognised that teams are not always like that. We spoke about what may need to be thought about in a team where there may be an absence of psychological safety.

Rosslyn

To me, it was rewarding to hear the appreciation for gaining a better understanding of each other. I have learned how unsafe and threatening it can feel to work in a context which is demanding and constantly changing. I was therefore particularly pleased that the exercise had felt anchoring. In considering our roots, with stories from our personal and professional histories, it felt that the values had meaning and were strengthened for us. This felt different to the way in which 'organisational values' can often be trotted off in a tokenistic way. Personally, it helps me as a manager to know that the ways in which we work and the decisions we make are located in these values. We are doing what we are doing for the right reasons. This helps me keep going when it can feel that we are feeling overwhelmed or unable to meet the needs we face daily.

Elizabeth

When doing individual trees and a team forest, we have found colleagues appreciating the chance to think about their stories, to hear others' stories and realise their connections and strength as a group as they added to each other's trees. As one person said, 'It has certainly given me confidence and made me feel part of the wider team. I thought being able to add what we valued about our colleagues to their trees was a moving way to express our gratitude, appreciation and acknowledgement for one another'. Our experience with a team tree was that it helped people from very different stages of their career connect, from undergraduate students to senior leaders: 'As an assistant psychologist... it was incredibly motivating to hear the stories of experienced psychologists and psychotherapists, how they became interested in the career, their passions and interests, as well as what it means to them to be a psychologist/psychotherapist. It was reassuring to be able to see that we shared similar values and goals'. Experienced colleagues shared being encouraged by the interest of those new to the work.

A few people over the years have found it more personal than they anticipated, and in one team, the manager started feeling responsible for the storms the team identified. So, as McParland and colleagues (2023) recommend, the facilitator needs to take a stand against 'blame turning up' and be clear that the aim is to understand each other better, and that people need to share only what they feel comfortable with. It is also important to stress that roots are about what sustains them, and not difficult early life experiences.

We have also used the Tree of Life with specific staff groups, such as assistant psychologists who have not got on to clinical psychology training (Elias and Field 2018), and with students and trainee health professionals coming to the end of placements or courses. For some of these workshops, there has been a training element where we have used the process of participating in the Tree of Life to introduce narrative therapy ideas, such as preferred story development. Chris and Keith, who you met in Chapter 8, shared their experience of problem-saturated stories of living with a dementia diagnosis alongside the preferred stories their trees helped them tell about how they live with the condition. Participants found the presence of Chris and Keith helped prompt different thinking about 'clients', with people commenting on the 'holistic' nature of the approach and feeling enabled to 'see people as people, not as a diagnosis'. Many described how the format of the workshop allowed them to understand the Tree of Life from the perspective of both the facilitator and the participant. Almost all participants shared their tree with family, friends or colleagues. They found the Tree of Life helped them see the bigger picture of how their work fitted with their life dreams and values, and for some sparked an interest in narrative therapy that has continued. Colleagues have taken their trees to appraisal and even an interview.

Supervision

As we see in the examples throughout this chapter, narrative practices can help staff develop their skills and knowledge in ways that align with their values and open new possibilities for actions and conversations. This holds true for us as well in our own supervision.

Jane

I have attended Hugh Fox's supervision group where we use outsider witness practices (Fox 2012; Fox, Tench and Marie 2002) in discussions about those we are working with. These conversations are recorded, so parts can be played to the client with the aim of contributing to their life, and their responses are brought back to the supervision group. In this way, all involved have their values and identities 'thickened' by having been heard and responded to. I feel like this supervision is an 'oasis' where I can return to support my clients and colleagues energised and 'topped up' with narrative ideas – vital when there has been no one else using narrative ideas in my service.

Conclusions

Our hopes in sharing some of this work with staff teams is to give you examples of how narrative techniques can be called upon in all the different types of work we do. Going further than that, we hope it has got you thinking a bit about why some of these experiences that our colleagues and we as writers face are so problematic. Returning to Vikki Reynolds's work on burnout, we can't help but think about how she highlights that burnout occurs when people become separated from their preferred identities and values. Staff members are often working in ways that feel unjust or make them feel disconnected from their personal values and the shared values they have among themselves. We hope we have shown you how various narrative practices can reconnect colleagues with their preferred identities and with each other. We find that these are perfectly placed to encourage conversation about some of these topics in a gentle but challenging way. Our experience is that people can and do feel differently about their work/experiences when given the space and support to do so.

Finally, for us as writers, the value we place on narrative therapy and techniques goes beyond how we see it as beneficial to others. We find ourselves thinking about our own stories, narratives and preferred identities and what we could be doing to live more in keeping with these. We find narrative practices help to sustain us. By working in ways that align with our values, and using these practices to thicken our own stories of what's important, we become more aware of the skills we have and the actions we can take to live in line with our preferred identities.

INVITATION TO REFLECT

- How do the exercises described here compare with your own experience of work meetings/supervision/awaydays? Do you think these ideas can add something useful?
- How do Vikki Reynolds's ideas about burnout fit for you? What might this mean for you in your work or for others you work with?

Useful resources

Denborough, D. (2008) *Collective Narrative Practice*. Adelaide: Dulwich Centre Publications.
Denborough, D. (2014) *Retelling the Stories of Our Lives: Everyday Narrative Therapy to Draw Inspiration and Transform Experience*. New York: W.W. Norton.
https://dulwichcentre.com.au
https://vikkireynolds.ca

CHAPTER 10

Ageing as Therapists

ACKNOWLEDGING OUR ANCESTORS AND LEAVING A LEGACY

Diane Clare
with contributions from Polly Kaiser, Rosslyn Offord and Elizabeth Field

Kia whakatōmuri te haere whakamua.
I walk backwards into the future with my eyes fixed on my past.
—WHAKATAUKĪ (MĀORI PROVERB)

Introduction

As we learned in Chapter 3, the stories or discourses of our lives are powerfully shaped by the wider stories within our communities and cultures. Different generations have all been affected by stories of what to expect about ageing. This differs across culture, gender and different levels of privilege and across time itself. These discourses can influence how we attempt to plan for our retirement. We see how stigma around mental health and dementia can constrain people, and as therapists working alongside older people, we often have conversations about retirement. As we have learned people may come to us with 'problem-saturated' stories about loss, such as those we read about in Chapter 4. This may be loss of meaning or status, loss of contact and connections, marital issues or financial constraints, and the various challenges that may bring. We have also shown how narrative practices can open new possibilities, new discourses and new identities. Narrative therapy invites us to notice unique outcomes (White and Epston 1990), whereby expected and well-worn paths of action and of identity can change, and so it is with ageing and retirement.

In this chapter, we invite you to reflect with us about your own ageing whether you consider yourself young and early on in your work; feel in the middle of it all, like Rosslyn and Elizabeth; are in a stage of transition or 'retirement', like Polly and me; or well into your later years. We hope this chapter gives you food for thought, whether that be for your own ageing or the conversations you have with others. As I write this in the context of Aotearoa New Zealand, the response to the ancestors, as in the proverb above, invites us to reflect on the legacies we carry from them.

Honouring our ancestors

In Aotearoa New Zealand, I am strongly influenced by Māori and Polynesian cultures and how they value their elders in a very positive way. This way of looking back at our histories is an important aspect of what we can draw on as we age: the wisdom of those who went before us. I do not have elders alive, but I have them in remembrance within – what Michael White (2007) refers to as a 'club of life'. When we look at our own ageing, this helps us connect again with our elders.

In our discussions as we prepared this book, we spoke of our ancestors, without whom we would not be here. For example, my father taught me the value of hard work, of making everything count for something and that there is no such word as *can't*. My mother, like my grandmother and great-grandmother, taught me the care of others, for being prepared to wait for that which may take time and to take a stand for what I believe in, even in the face of strong opposition, and to be an activist for causes where those without voices can be heard. My aunties reminded me of the balance of good humour and learning to respond to what matters, saying 'life is too short to bother with petty things'.

Elizabeth has in her head her father saying, 'a Christian never retires'; a grandmother who ran mother and toddler groups on a local estate well into her 80s; and a mother she admires for always being warm and welcoming whatever challenges she faces as she ages.

Rosslyn's branch of Suffolk ancestry honours eccentricity – a distant uncle who wore a top hat and lived in a hollow tree, and Great Uncle Herb, who retired at 50 to travel the world, lived out his naturist tendencies in the sun and looked after stray dogs. Alongside this there is a legacy of community involvement. Rosslyn's grandparents were active in their communities into their 80s. Following in their footsteps, her parents recently received a community award for their support of children and young people and the cultural life of the village. Her dad is most proud of a local craft beer being named in his honour!

Polly is influenced by her 'pioneer' family in the United States, the courage of her great-grandmothers and her mother. One of her greatest influences is her 90-year-old aunt who raised ten children, and then, using all her experiences volunteering with peace and social justice groups, started work setting up an international non-violent peace force. While she no longer works with them day-to-day, she is still very much an activist and has influenced Polly's own motivation in community endeavours.

Discourses on retirement

Beliefs about retirement vary. They might be very ambivalent or be a relief and sense of liberty, or they may be something dreaded with fears of being 'obsolete' and 'on the shelf'. We four are all clinical psychologists who have worked in health services, including the NHS. Our cultural influences differ covering American, French, Māori, English, Irish and Welsh, and our ages range from 50s to 70s. We recognise the privileged positions we are in, in this regard, in having choices that many do not. Ageing is, sadly, not a luxury afforded to all. Some may need to end their work due to illness or to become carers, and discourses of redundancy or 'forced retirement' may be different. However, we want to explore the question: what is the process of ending for therapists, especially for those of us who work with older people?

We have seen in previous chapters, particularly Chapter 7, how the use of the outsider witness might apply in a range of settings – with clients, in communities and to support colleagues. We wondered if it might be a helpful way to begin to explore our own ageing as therapists. Thus, building on several years of conversations about the 'R' word with

Polly and me, Rosslyn interviewed us both by facilitating our reflections, with Elizabeth taking an outsider witness position. Here, we share some of the conversation we had in relation to reflections on discourses on retirement, to build on the connections between us and thicken our preferred stories. You will see how moving back and forth between present and past, weaving in our cultural and family stories and sharing resonances all thicken our preferred stories of us as therapists and as people.

> **INVITATION TO REFLECT**
> We invite you to listen, in the hope this may spark some ideas of your own. What are the discourses on ageing, retirement, later life and being old that are influencing you? Think about where these might come from: family, culture, religion? What are your values and how might they influence how you spend your later years?

Stories of work

We started our conversation with Rosslyn inviting us to reflect on our career paths.

Diane: My decision to enter the profession of clinical psychology stemmed from life experiences of trauma and loss. In 1979, one of my four children died at a young age of 3 years and 5 months after a life of struggle with his health. Mark was a warrior who taught me more in those short years than any training before or since. He helped me to learn about the voices of the voiceless, the enablement of the disabled and a better way that we can offer help. Consequently, people and their families can tell their stories of ordinary lives and leave this world with us knowing of their extraordinary contribution to this path of life, however long or short it may be. Based on what Mark taught me, I would often reflect that 'there must be a better way than this' in terms of how we respond to the needs of others in health services. I learned that healthcare across all ages requires a different way of being with people, so they feel met, seen, heard and held in ways not always offered by all health practitioners.

In time, I was to become enchanted by the narrative approach (Hedtke 2003; Hedtke and Winslade 2004; White 1988, 1995, 2000; White and Epston 1990; Wingard 1998). Re-membering practices give a space to reflect how the gift that Mark gave me, like my older ancestors had given me, was not left behind. This is how we honour our ancestors and enrich our pathway, no matter what our role, and it is a pathway of hope and legacy as we approach life, work and, later, retirement.

Polly: My motivations for narrative therapy come from my own lived experiences of difficulty, trauma and dislocations (by the age of one, I had lived next to the Pacific, the Atlantic and the Mediterranean). From my parents and grandparents, I learned the importance of treating people well. As an undergraduate, I was taught by John Shotter, a social constructionist, who led me to the works of Ken Gergen, where I learned theory about discourses and how stories are of a time and place (Gergen 1973). I just never knew how to translate these values into my therapy until the light bulb moment when Hugh Fox gave me Michael White's paper 'Saying Hullo' (1988), which validated in print what I had secretly been doing for years (Kaiser 2008). I owe a great deal to listening to my clients and from workshops with Hugh and Michael over the years.

Stories of physical ageing

Polly and I shared how we talked together for some years about our experiences of getting older and the impact on the body and mind as well as how life and work changed.

Polly: Studying the psychology and spirituality of ageing has been one thing, but as I have aged my body has become less reliable. Ridiculously, I totally underestimated the effects of age on the body. So, looking back on my conversations with clients, I wonder if I was sympathetic enough. I talked about pacing with them, but did I do that myself?

Rosslyn: Can you say more about what it was like to notice, having underestimated the physical aspects of ageing, and what that might mean for how you thought about your clients? And what it meant for yourself to notice your body starting to let you down?

Polly: Yes, when I was younger, exercise seemed to be about conforming to being slim and beautiful, but I rebelled against these messages. If I had been told to keep fit so I could climb mountains with my children and grandchildren, I might have taken more notice! I cannot go up the mountain with my kids any more, but I am so glad I can still swim in lochs, rivers and oceans.

Rosslyn: So, it came up about gendered discourses as a younger woman?

Polly: Yes, absolutely! Diane is a great role model for me as she has a bloomin' gym in her garage!

Diane: I got the gym to help keep me fit, but it is also helping with my ageing to strengthen my knees.

Rosslyn: So, tell me what was connecting for you in what Polly was saying, or is there a different experience for you around this and how it feels for your body as it ages?

Diane: Age can surprise us much earlier than anticipated. Polly and I both note how nobody ever told us about our knees as we age, so the body tells us before our minds are ready. I realised in my 50s how arthritis slowed me down long before I expected it. Near our house was the number 51 bus which chugged up the hill, and I recall telling my daughter how I felt like that 51 bus. She said she hoped it would be one of those buses that has velvet seats and that kneels for you to step onto it, which I found beautiful and so comforting. For me, based on my ancestors' experiences, I expected that I would work and then stop, and there would be no gradation. Then I recognised that life is different now to my parents' lives, and this is partly due to the opportunities offered by my professional role. As I am now self-employed, I can slowly let go of work and adjust to a slower pace rather than stop abruptly. This in turn allows me to reshape that discourse and be creative about what retirement looks like.

Stories of retirement

We then moved on in our conversation to consider the stories we have about retirement. As therapists, we talk about the concept of endings, and there are discourses about how therapy generally 'should' conclude. Fredman and Dalal (1998) note that there are interplays of political climate, agency context and funding that influence the ending discourse for us, along with our beliefs, and how we frame all that in the therapeutic relationship. They speak of ending in therapy in terms of a loss, as a cure, as a transition and often as a relief or a metamorphosis. So, as we work through the layers of loss, of release/cure, of transition and relief in endings, perhaps we must apply this to our own process for retiring.

Diane: I felt relief in ending my work with health services, although I am continuing to engage in work that is influenced by all those years. However, work reduces as ageing dictates and so those elements of loss, of cure, of transition, of relief and, indeed, of metamorphosis are similar for therapists.

Polly: I needed to retire after a health issue and, while I felt relief at the end of all the bureaucracy, I still felt guilty about leaving my team and colleagues. I worked some more in a regional role as part of my transition before doing what I do now. Given my ancestors and role models, I am not sure when I will ever fully stop.

Rosslyn: Can you say more? As it is making me think about stuff we are doing in Britain, and I'm not sure if it is the same in New Zealand about not mandating retirement, but earlier when you said, Diane, that at some point we must stop, what does that mean for you?

Diane: In New Zealand, we have what is called the 'Golden Oldie' card that you get at age 65, so even if still working you are entitled to things like having a free pass on the train at certain times of day and other discounts. When my father retired, he got the gold watch to finish his working life, and this is different. I see this as a kind of rite of passage for me and not a finality.

Polly: I think that I am a workaholic like my father, who worked until the day before he died. I must watch that, as I would have continued, but I had a clot, and a friend dropped dead around that time with a clot on her lungs. That shocked me into thinking: I have got to stop! It still took me 9 months, a kind of gestation period from the realisation of needing to end work for the NHS. And even then, I carried on for just over a year working regionally. Now, I am beginning to experience it as liberating. It gives me time to do other things that are creative with poetry and writing in the community and pottery. It was great to know that no one can sack me, and I can choose what work I do. This change for me was a springboard for the work I do now with Mature Minds Matter (see Chapter 8).

Rosslyn: Diane, you previously spoke of the rite of passage and moving from working for a big employer to working for yourself, and in ways you both have continued working. Coming back to discourses about retirement and what ageing is supposed to look like, you both have ideas about doing lots of stuff and having things going on in your life?

Diane: I am seeing retirement differently to Polly as it is less about doing things in the community and more about using the knowledge I bring with me and my experience. I have seen a big shift since I decided to let retirement be a word I said aloud. When I turned 70, the 'R' word came in, and I decided on a gradual reduction in elements of work, which was a kind of wow for me realising it is not sudden death. It is different, with a different landscape of identity and a very different landscape of action.

Polly: Yes, it is a difference, and we both have transformed from health service employment to our different paths.

This led to conversations about these future paths and turned to what this new stage might be like in terms of legacies, illustrated by this quote: 'Ageing is not lost youth but a new stage of opportunity and strength' Betty Friedan (1993, p.110).

Stories of future hopes and legacies

Rosslyn: Can I ask more about leaving something of value to others as I think this resonates with you too Polly?

Polly: Yes, absolutely. I think that is part of my motivation for this book – sharing and leaving some concrete ideas and legacy – which is why it is such an honour to work with both of you. Yes, so passing something on for me is this book, other papers and the Greater Manchester Mature Minds Matter. This is a growing network of older people in Greater Manchester with lived experience that brings people together for them to input into the NHS and other ageing initiatives. All my life has been about helping to bring people together, so they have a voice and a place to connect, be that in a post-natal group, a park group, a local dementia charity group or even my local choir.

Rosslyn: I could feel my interest peaking when you both talked about what might connect for you both. I wonder about things for you, Diane, and what connected with you about leaving something for others to keep going?

Diane: My mother died when she had lived only half her life at age 54, and it was a difficult time. I think of her to this day. I think Mum would have been so excited about what I have done with my life. When I was a teen, she gave me a card which said, 'Just believe in yourself and whatever you want to be, and you will be able to do it'. It meant the world to me. My dad was always on the go and a workaholic, whereas Mum was a kind and gentle soul in the background, encouraging me. There is something about remembering a mum who never got old too, and all she lived through – including the Blitz in London, surviving nearly 5 years with my dad at war – and what a different life and different expectations of life they had. Whereas for me, I am privileged to live longer, and I am thinking of the greater opportunities for my children and grandchildren too. In my work, I have an investment in the younger generation and the task they must pick up with the lack of investment in services in New Zealand, as it is in Britain. So, a lot of the community activities Polly speaks about with such excitement are so helpful and hopeful. Grassroots groups are powerful, and I am thinking of gifting something back when I retire to our local women's community services. I could bring something to that, and I will also write more, support others and teach. Leaving something of value for others to pick up, I find that quite exciting. I have a colleague who is 30 who I have encouraged to present her work at conferences. I have done my dash, so now it is her turn!

Polly: Connection is vital for me and for my clients, so now I do not see them one-to-one. I teach and write and provide workshops, which I love. Our clients often come to us disconnected, don't they? Disconnected from themselves, or a daughter they want to have a closer relationship with, or a husband, or a community. What I love about narrative therapy is that it helps build that connection. The values I have from my family and as a therapist are all about connection. That is why I like the groups where we provide spaces which help people to build their own relationships and connections. I've just remembered that the South Asian elder work I did was called 'Making Connections, Not Assumptions', and I still maintain some of those connections.

Retelling reflections

Rosslyn: I want to say how moving I found that last part and all the things it sparked off for me. Elizabeth, having listened to Diane and Polly sharing their experiences of ageing as narrative therapists, was there a particular phrase or idea that had resonance for you?

Elizabeth: Quite a lot of things stood out for me. I was drawn to comments of things they had not anticipated and how my joints also ached sooner than I expected. Both used the word 'connection', which resonated for me. That is something of value that runs through my work too. I too want to honour parents and ancestors in a familial sense and those who came before me in my work context.

Rosslyn: The ancestors and those who have gone before, personally and workwise – is this about connection for you?

Elizabeth: Connection as a kind of dance came to mind. In their conversation, lots of contradictions came up in terms of connection and stopping. There was connection and disconnection which made me think of a dance: one step forward, one back, and maybe to the side and maybe step together and maybe dance with somebody else.

Rosslyn: Listening to Polly and Diane, is there something you would like to say as in the dance image and the stop-and-start movement?

Elizabeth: What I like about the dance metaphor is the delight with initial connections and how some last a long time and some are quite brief. Polly talked about that with things she had set up and continued with for years, and others she started up and had less long-term involvement. I think in our work we often offer people connections that are not long, but there is still delight and value in those connections that can be deep even if they are short.

Rosslyn: So, where might that take you, and has the conversation changed for you with this?

Elizabeth: Listening to Polly and Diane, who are part of the connections I made early in my career, made me think about wanting to help colleagues with their next career steps – and being quite evangelical when they want to work with older people. When they talked about their parents, I was struck by how much people in their 60s and 70s are still talking about their parents, which I found interesting as both a daughter and a mother.

Retelling of the retelling

This telling was a rich reflection of our ages and stages across our work as therapists, which took us back to our ancestors in honouring ways. In her reflections, Polly mentioned Maya Angelou referring to her ancestors on her shoulders and how she brings them into the room with her. I so loved Elizabeth speaking of her 'evangelical work' in supporting the next generation to work with older people. Rosslyn spoke of a Welsh phrase: *Gwnewch y pethau bychain* – 'Do the small things'. For me, understanding ageing and retirement is such a big topic, but it helps me to remember that the small things are such an important part of this journey too, and they sow seeds for the future.

Conclusions

I reflected on the positive strength and opportunity I had come to value as I got older, whereas when younger I saw retirement as something somewhat fearful or negative. For me, based on my ancestors' experiences, I expected there would be no gradation. Now, I am caught out with sparkling moments and realise that some of us can change those prescriptions to a gentler transition.

Beyond the therapy room, I offer a legacy of learning from my clients' journeys of transformation and reclamation in my writing, supervision and teaching. This is a liberation that Polly and I share as we move forward, and this has a movement that is no longer a threat but flows into landscapes of opportunity and new discoveries about identity. Opportunities I now see are the choice to retire which, as mentioned, is a privilege not available to all. I deeply value the chance to gradate my retirement pathway rather than a sudden-death type of ending. This parallels the gradual ageing process we face where the body dictates and becomes the boss, and for me, I have a love–hate relationship with my bossy body now! As Polly recently reminded me, quoting Bette Davis, 'Old age ain't no place for sissies!'

We can overcome the fear of becoming obsolete or out of date and even of physical decline and lost independence if we see the next stepping stone and put in place our networks of support and connection. I have slowly learned to let go of some things and continue with others, opening space for a comfort level that the 'R' word so restricted for me in my 50s and towards my 60s. Covid-19 taught us to travel virtually, so that is one thing that came out of that terrible pandemic which now gives me hope for connection with friends and family despite these restrictions.

Once we grasp these threats as challenges for our creativity to adapt, we can smile at the dawn of a new day with time for our partner, for friendships and for family without work getting in the way. No epitaph says, 'I wish I had spent more time at work', but we might wish for more sunrises. However, those who come next *are* those sunrises and the promise of something awesome.

A few months after our conversation, in October 2024, I saw my last therapy clients. This is what I wrote to Polly, Rosslyn and Elizabeth:

Yesterday the door closed on 43 years of therapy work. It was a full and emotional day for me with the last clients using their sessions to reflect on our journeys and, wow, so amazing. It was one of those rainy days you get in spring in Aotearoa which was very overcast and broody – a good reflection of the emotions of the day.

One client said she loved me to bits for having prompted her to make the changes she had never made in over 70 years of her life – so another wow as she clearly had a spring in her step as she left and was so ready to move on now and do amazing things.

There was something hugely challenging about leaving my key behind – never coming back to sit in that space again. Lots to process but I feel it is complete.

Then we had a meal out with our daughter, and she was a baby when I started this *mahi* [work]. It hit home for her when she gasped, 'Forty-three years: that is my entire life!' Yup, and in many ways, it has been mine.

So, I slept in the next day, had a long sleep and a slow start with nobody due for supervision all day, so it is good to just go aaahhh in relief. Space is opening for Tuesdays to be Choose Days for me, as that is the only therapy day I had remaining, and now it is morphing into something completely different.

Some final thoughts and suggestions for you, the reader

Having had a taste of our conversations you may like to consider your own responses to ageing and retirement. For me, this shifted across my 50s, 60s and now my 70s, and these lost identities and landscapes of action have made me adjust. I think five-yearly reflections on this journey will be interesting as I head towards 75 and beyond. As we ask our clients about their goals for therapy and how things might seem or feel for when they finish therapy, we could apply this to ourselves regardless of the role we play. We could ask: what do you hope to feel, to do and to enjoy when you retire, and what will bring you joy?

In many ways, this discussion has drawn on all the elements of the Tree of Life metaphor (Ncube 2007a, 2007b) where we acknowledge our roots and what has led us to the skills and interests we have in the trunk of our being. We have spoken of the branches of our hopes and dreams and weathered the storms along the way. As part of this we spoke of the fruits and gifts given to us and the people of importance to us: evergreen or fallen leaves. It is so helpful to recognise the ground of our present life as we reflect on our Tree of Life.

For us, taking time to reflect on our work and life stages has made us think about those who came before us, those who come alongside us and those who will come after. It has had us thinking about passing knowledge from generation to generation, and about the discourses that shape our stories. Our hope for this chapter, sharing our reflections on getting older and changing our relationship to work and retirement, is that you will be better positioned to notice the discourses impacting you and those you work and live with, so you can make choices more in keeping with your values.

Reflecting on Rosslyn's Welsh saying about doing the small things, here in conclusion is a Māori whakataukī (proverb):

Mai i te purapura iti rawa Ka tupu ko te tino rākau.
From the smallest seed grows the mightiest of trees.

Afterword

Polly Kaiser, Rosslyn Offord and Elizabeth Field

We would like to thank you for joining us in our exploration of the ways in which narrative practice can be helpful in supporting older people and people living with dementia. As editors, we have been inspired, excited and deeply moved by the stories our authors and contributors have shared with us, and it has felt like an immense privilege to be given permission to include these in our book. We hope that this book has been helpful to you whether you are reading this as a student or practitioner, a researcher, an older person or a carer.

We would like to finish our book by briefly returning to some of the themes and ideas that have shone out through the writing and which feel important to underline before drawing to a close.

The psychological consequences of poverty, abuse, discrimination, stigma and ageism are visible and debilitating. We see the consequences of these in our therapy rooms, and you have been able to read about their impact on older people's mental health. Some chapters have been co-written alongside people who have come to see us, like Karen, Viv and Chris, and the voices of many others are woven through each chapter. We are thankful to them all as this 'keeps it real'. Just as honesty is an important value for Maeve, so too with us. The power of individual therapy to help people overcome the psychological legacies of historical disempowerment is limited. However, much of the attraction of narrative practices is the way these legacies can begin to be challenged. As you can see, they have certainly made a difference to our lives and the lives of clients and colleagues alike.

Throughout this book, you will see questions developed by narrative therapists like Michael White, David Epston and others. We have asked questions and invited you to reflect on how certain ideas and stories connect with you. In Chapter 6, which was actually the first to be written, Karen said to Rosslyn, 'You ask the right questions.' This enabled her to tell her story in such a powerful way, so that when Polly read it, she immediately wished she could give it to every carer she had ever seen! She felt as if Karen's story encapsulated so many issues that she had heard from carers over the past 40 years. It is concerning/distressing that, despite much progress around dementia, these stories are still being told today. That is why this book is so important. Our hope is that you too will be able to be curious, ask the 'right questions' and support people to tell their stories that need to be heard.

As editors, we have been struck by how often the stories shared in this book have referenced the power of discourses, or 'rules for living', to shape how people see themselves. In Chapter 3, we discussed the ways in which ageism intersects with factors such as gender, race and class to create different expectations for how lives should be lived. We also bear witness to the impact of poverty and inequality. As we have worked on the different chapters, we have reflected on how vital these factors are in understanding psychological distress. We have tried to acknowledge this in different ways throughout the book, being conscious of the ways in which our own experiences and perceptions are shaped by these factors too. We have tried to acknowledge the limits of our own perspectives as therapists, writers and editors. We hope that we have shared the ways in which narrative therapy can give us tools to work with these issues in a meaningful way.

We would like to comment in particular about what we have noticed around expectations about gender roles, which can seem different when working with an older population. This hasn't always been explicitly named but seemed to us highly relevant and implicit in understanding, for example, expectations about caring that women may hold, while men may have ideas around different roles and responsibilities in life. It seemed to us that this was relevant in every story we have read!

Taking a stand against the failures of more conventional mainstream psychological therapies to address these social and political issues can often feel like a lonely position. Narrative practice has helped us to navigate some of these challenges. Importantly, it intentionally connects us with others, and this has been one of the joys of writing this book together as a collective. It also gives us a framework for understanding the distress often felt by us and our colleagues, working in systems that are under extreme pressure, and offers us ways of working through this – together. We hope that this emphasis on the importance of connection and solidarity has been made clear and brought to life for you.

These values do not appear from nowhere. In Chapters 8 and 10 we talked about the Tree of Life metaphor, which is one that has guided us in our initial coming together and in writing this book. All of us, as authors, have our roots in wanting to make a difference and to help people in an ethical way that supports our values, such as care, commitment, connecting, making a difference, standing up to injustice, challenging stigma and being creative. We each have our own individual stories, and we have shared snippets with you, especially in the last chapter. Depending on where they are in our own 'club of life', our ancestors and predecessors have, undoubtably, taught us all so much, whether it is to follow in their footsteps or know where not to tread! We may not always question where our values come from, but many of us feel it when we work in ways that are not congruent with them. As we have read, the environments we work in can so often work against connection. Systems and injustices can rub uncomfortably against our values. Thus, the importance of Chapter 9 on supporting ourselves and our colleagues.

As we said in our introduction, most (but not all) of us are White psychologists working in the NHS, and we write from a particular context at a particular time. There continues to be an under-representation of voices from people of colour, especially within NHS psychological therapy settings, among both people who access our services and therapists. Many of us are involved in work that seeks to address this injustice. We hope that as we find more helpful ways to connect with colleagues and service users from a greater range of communities, our work will reflect this greater diversity.

We have all learned the importance of listening out for the ways in which faith and spirituality may contribute to identity, connections and hopes for life, as we heard about in Ron's story. This is something in our often-secular society that we can miss as therapists. Yet it may be vital to talk about with older people and people living with dementia who are grappling with the existential issues that emerge as they consider what it means to be nearing the end of their life.

It is often in our community settings and working alongside colleagues in the voluntary sector that we may have the freedom to use some of the wonderful creative approaches described in Chapter 8. We hope that wherever you work – community, inpatient, memory services, voluntary sector or as carers and interested older people – you may find some good ideas to develop.

We had many discussions on how to 'slice the cake' that is this book – what chapters, and where and how our stories can best be organised. While we have separate chapters on loss and trauma, these stories weave through other chapters, such as when Karen talks about her grief at not being at the birth of her grandchild, or how Thomas's anxieties were connected with the death of his wife 18 months prior to Helen seeing him.

The context of retirement has also felt to us very present in many stories we have shared, such as in Joe's motivation to volunteer as an outsider witness, or the discourses about how retirement should look that Karen refers to. Retiring as therapists provided the context for our final chapter, which we hope is of assistance to you as a reader of any age in considering your hopes for how you may approach your own ageing.

As editors, we have discussed how we wish we had had this book when we started out! We have already found it helpful. We have been given fresh ideas to take back to the places we live and work, and each of us has been reminded of our roots and our values and reconnected with ideas that help to ground us going forward. Our hope is that this book will help your endeavours too. We sincerely hope that it encourages the spirit of adventure, curiosity and creativity that Michael White and David Epston first wrote about. We have loved reading about the 'sparkling moments'. We began hoping that our book would be a way of connecting people and building on these wonderful ideas, and we would really love to hear from you if you are working in these ways.

As we end our book we come full circle, and hope that we have honoured our intentions to challenge stigma, support connection and build hope. The project of writing and editing this book has given us fresh hope, and we hope that this has been your experience too.

INVITATION TO REFLECT

We invite you to use outsider witness questions as you reflect on the stories and ideas in this book.

- As you have read, what stories or ideas have you been drawn to? Which values have stood out to you?
- What came to mind as you read? Any images start to form in your mind?
- What is it about your own experiences that meant these ideas and stories captured you? Any thoughts of who you might want to connect with?
- Where has reading this book taken you? What might you do now having read this book? Might there be ways that you can build on the connections you have, whether through friends, family, neighbours or colleagues, or build new ones? Do you feel you have ways of linking up with other people that help to anchor you and keep you in touch with your preferences and hopes for your life?

WRITERS WORKSHOP; MANCHESTER JULY 2023.
FRONT ROW: HELEN, POLLY, ROSSLYN. MIDDLE ROW: GEMMA, ELIZABETH, JANE. BACK: SARA.

References

Aman, J. (2006) 'Therapist as host: Making my guests feel welcome'. *International Journal of Narrative Therapy and Community Work 3*, 3-10.

American Psychological Association (2020) *APA Resolution on Ageism*. www.apa.org/about/policy/resolution-ageism.pdf

Applewhite, A. (2016) *This Chair Rocks: A Manifesto Against Ageism*. Padstow: TJ International.

Aries, P. (1982) *The Hour of Our Death: The Classic History of Western Attitudes Toward Death Over the Last One Thousand Years (2nd ed.)*. New York: Random House.

Arulampalam, S., Perera, L., de Mel, S., White, C. and Denborough, D. (2006) 'Avoiding psychological colonisation: Stories from Sri Lanka – responding to the tsunami'. In D. Denborough (ed.), *Trauma: Narrative Responses to Traumatic Experience*. Adelaide: Dulwich Centre Publications.

Bartlett, R. and O'Connor, D. (2010) *Broadening the Dementia Debate: Towards Social Citizenship*. Bristol: Policy Press.

Beels, C. (2009) 'Some historical conditions of narrative work'. *Family Process 48*, 3, 363-378.

Besley, A.C. (2002) 'Foucault and the turn to narrative therapy'. *British Journal of Guidance & Counselling 30*, 2, 125-143.

Blake, D. and Kaiser, P. (2019) '"It reminds you really of what the job is about": Introducing narrative practices to an older adult day hospital'. *FPOP Bulletin: Psychology of Older People 145*, 47-52.

Bostock, J. (2017) 'Understanding power in order to share hope: A tribute to David Smail'. *Clinical Psychology Forum 293*, 32-35.

Boyle, M. and Johnstone L. (2020) *A Straight Talking Introduction to the Power Threat Meaning Framework*. Manchester: PCCS Books.

Burr, V. (2003) *Social Constructionism (2nd ed.)*. London and New York: Routledge.

Butler, R.N. (1969) 'Age-ism: Another form of bigotry'. *The Gerontologist 9*, 4(1), 243-246.

Cain, S. (2013) *Quiet: The Power of Introverts in a World That Can't Stop Talking*. London: Penguin.

Carey, M., Walther, M.A. and Russell, S. (2009) 'The absent but implicit: A map to support therapeutic enquiry'. *Family Process 48*, 3, 319-331.

Chaplin, R., Farquharson, L., Clapp, M. and Crawford, M. (2015) 'Comparison of access, outcomes and experiences of older adults and working age adults in psychological therapy'. *International Journal of Geriatric Psychiatry 30*, 178-184.

Clark, A. (2015) 'Pat Barker interview: "I'm edgy, but not dead pigeon sort of edgy"'. *The Guardian*, 29 August 2015.

Cohen, L. (1992) 'Anthem' [Song]. On album *The Future*. Sony Music.

Combs, G. and Freedman, J. (2004) *A Poststructuralist Approach to Narrative Work: The Handbook of Narrative and Psychotherapy*. London: SAGE.

Combs, G. and Freedman, J. (2016) 'Narrative therapy's relational understanding of identity'. *Family Process* 55, 2, 211–224.

Dall'Ora, C., Ball, J., Reinius, M. and Griffiths, P. (2020) 'Burnout in nursing: A theoretical review'. *Human Resources for Health* 18, 1, 41.

Davies, J. (2021) *Sedated: How Modern Capitalism Created Our Mental Health Crisis*. London: Atlantic Books.

Denborough, D. (2008) *Collective Narrative Practice: Responding to Individuals, Groups, and Communities Who Have Experienced Trauma*. Adelaide: Dulwich Centre Publications.

Denborough, D. (2009) 'Some reflections on the legacies of Michael White: An Australian perspective'. *Australian and New Zealand Journal of Family Therapy* 30, 2, 92–108.

Denborough, D. (2012) 'A storyline of collective narrative practice: A history of ideas, social projects, and partnerships'. *International Journal of Narrative Therapy and Community Work* 1, 40–65.

Denborough, D. (2014) *Retelling the Stories of Our Lives: Everyday Narrative Therapy to Draw Inspiration and Transform Experience*. New York: W.W. Norton.

Eerola, P., Paananen, M. and Repo, K. (2023) '"Ordinary" and "diverse" families: A case study of family discourses by Finnish early childhood education and care administrators'. *Journal of Family Studies* 29, 2, 489–505.

Elias, L. and Field, E. (2018) 'Tree of Life workshop for assistant psychologists working with older people: My reflections'. *FPOP Bulletin: Psychology of Older People* 141, 66–67.

Felitti, V.J., Anda, R.F., Nordenberg, D., Williamson, D.F. et al. (1998) 'Adverse childhood experiences'. *American Journal of Preventive Medicine* 14, 4, 245–258. doi:10.1016/S0749-3797(98)00017-8

Field, E. (2017) 'Tree of Life Project in NHS Mental Health Services for Older People'. Unpublished diploma paper, Institute of Narrative Therapy. https://theint.co.uk/wp-content/uploads/2019/07/elizfieldfinal.pdf

Foucault, M. (1980) *Power/Knowledge: Selected Interviews and Other Writings, 1972–1977* (C. Gordon, ed.). New York: Pantheon Books.

Fox, H. (2003) *Developing Skills in Narrative Therapy* [Internal training workshop for Pennine Care NHS Foundation Trust], June.

Fox, H. (2012) *On Using Narrative Ideas in Supervision*. Adelaide: Dulwich Centre Publications.

Fox, H., Tench, C. and Marie (2002) 'Outsider-witness practices and group supervision'. *International Journal of Narrative Therapy and Community Work* 4, 25–32.

Fraser, J., Williams, L., Hayes, M., Akpan, U. and Bowerman, U. (2018) 'Humanising the inpatient experience through service user-led Tree of Life workshops'. *Clinical Psychology Forum* 3, 12, 7–13.

Fredman, G. and Dalal, C. (1998) 'Ending discourses: Implications for relationships and action in therapy'. *Human Systems: The Journal of Systemic Consultation and Management* 9, 1, 1–13.

Freedman, J. and Combs, G. (1996) *Narrative Therapy: The Social Construction of Preferred Realities*. London and New York: W.W. Norton.

Friedan, B. (1993) *The Fountain of Age*. New York: Simon & Schuster.

Gergen, K.J. (1973) 'Social psychology as history'. *Journal of Personality and Social Psychology* 26, 309–320.

Gergen, K.J. (1985) 'The social constructionist movement in modern psychology'. *American Psychologist* 40, 266–275.

Gergen, K.J. (2009) *Realities and Relationships: Soundings in Social Construction*. Cambridge, MA: Harvard University Press.

Goldsmith, M. (2004) *Ageing, Spirituality and Well-Being*. London: Jessica Kinglsey Publishers.

Greenwood, D. (2023) 'The eight advantages'. http://coachingasperger.com/advantages
Guilfoyle, M. (2015) 'Listening in narrative therapy: Double listening and empathic positioning'. *South African Journal of Psychology 45*, 1, 36- 49. doi:10.1177/0081246314556711
Hayward, M. (2009) 'Is narrative therapy systemic?' *Context*, October, 13–16.
Hedtke, L. (2003) 'The origami of re-membering'. *International Journal of Narrative Therapy and Community Work 4*, 57–62.
Hedtke, L. and Winslade, J. (2004) *Re-membering Lives and Conversations with the Dying and the Bereaved*. Amityville, NY: Baywood Publishing.
Hoffman, L. (1990) 'Constructing realities: An art of lenses'. *Family Process 29*, 1–12.
Holland, S. (1992) 'From social abuse to social action: A neighbourhood psychotherapy and social action project for women'. In J. Ussher and P. Nicholson (eds), *Gender Issues in Clinical Psychology*. London: Routledge.
Holman, D. and Walker, A. (2021) 'Understanding unequal ageing: Towards a synthesis of intersectionality and life course analyses'. *European Journal of Ageing 18*, 2, 239–255.
Holmgren, K., Hensing, G. and Dahlin-Ivanoff, S. (2009) 'Development of a questionnaire assessing work-related stress in women – Identifying individuals who risk being put on sick leave'. *Disability and Rehabilitation 31*, 4, 284–292.
Horne, D. (2024) *Dawn's Dementia Field Guide*. Canterbury, UK: Lioness Writing.
Jeffery, S. (2024) *Deconstructing Ageing: A Workbook for Continuing Professional Development and Reflexivity*. Manchester: Greater Manchester Mental Health NHS Foundation Trust.
Jennings, L. (ed.) (2014) *Welcome to Our World: A Collection of Life Writing by People Living with Dementia*. Canterbury, UK: Forget-Me-Nots.
Jennings, L. (ed.) (2020) *Time and Place: Collected Poems*. Canterbury, UK: Lioness Writing.
Johnson, J., Culverwell, A., Hulbert, S., Roberton, M. and Camic, P.M. (2015) 'Museum activities in dementia care: Using visual analogue scales to measure subjective well-being'. *Dementia 16*, 5, 591–610. doi:10.1177/1471301215611763
Johnstone, L. and Boyle, M. (2018) 'The power threat meaning framework: An alternative nondiagnostic conceptual system'. *Journal of Humanistic Psychology*. https://doi.org/10.1177/0022167818793289
Johnstone, L. and Boyle, M. with Cromby, J., Dillon, J., Harper, D., Kinderman, P. et al. (2018) *The Power Threat Meaning Framework: Towards the Identification of Patterns in Emotional Distress, Unusual Experiences and Troubled or Troubling Behaviour, as an Alternative to Functional Psychiatric Diagnosis*. Leicester: BPS Books.
Joseph Rowntree Foundation (2017) *UK Poverty 2017*. York: JRF. www.jrf.org.uk/report/uk-poverty-2017
Kaiser, P. (2008) '"You say goodbye and I say hello": Narrative therapy and remembering practices with older people'. *PSIGE Newsletter 104*.
Kaiser, P. (2017a) 'End of life care'. In P. Kaiser and R. Eley (eds), *Life Story Work with People with Dementia: Ordinary Lives, Extraordinary People*. London: Jessica Kingsley Publishers.
Kaiser, P. (2017b) 'Narrative approaches to life story work'. In P. Kaiser and R. Eley (eds), *Life Story Work with People with Dementia: Ordinary Lives, Extraordinary People*. London: Jessica Kingsley Publishers.
Kaiser, P. and Blake, D. (2022) 'Listening for stories of trauma and stories of hope with older people'. *Context 181*, June, 36–38.
Kaiser, P. and Eley, R. (eds) (2017) *Life Story Work with People with Dementia: Ordinary Lives, Extraordinary People*. London: Jessica Kingsley Publishers.
Kaseke, S. (2010) 'Standing together on a riverbank: Group conversations about sexual abuse in Zimbabwe'. *International Journal of Narrative Therapy and Community Work 4*, 42–44.

Keady, J., Williams, S. and Hughes-Roberts, J. (2007) 'Making mistakes: Using co-constructed inquiry to illuminate meaning and relationships in the early adjustment to Alzheimer's disease: A single case study approach'. *Dementia 6*, 343–364.

Kis-Sines, N. and Pluznik, R. (2014) 'Tree of Life: Questions about professional identity for child and youth workers'. https://dulwichcentre.com.au/wp-content/uploads/2014/01/tree-of-life-professional-identity.pdf

Kitwood, T. (1997) *Dementia Reconsidered: The Person Comes First* ('Rethinking Ageing' Series). Buckingham: Open University Press.

Kitwood, T. and Bredin, K. (1992) 'Towards a theory of dementia care: Personhood and well-being'. *Ageing & Society 12*, 3, 269–287.

Kiyimba, N., Buxton, C., Shuttleworth, J. and Pathe, E. (2022) *Discourses of Psychological Trauma*. Palgrave Macmillan/Springer Nature. https://doi.org/10.1007/978-3-031-07711-1

Koenig, H.G., McCullough, M.E. and Larson, D.B. (2001) *Handbook of Religion and Health*. Oxford: Oxford University Press.

Koppel, J. and Rubin, D.C. (2016) 'Recent advances in understanding the reminiscence bump: The importance of cues in guiding recall from autobiographical memory'. *Current Directions in Psychological Science 25*, 2, 135–140. https://doi.org/10.1177/0963721416631955

Kübler-Ross, E. (1969) *On Death and Dying*. New York: Macmillan.

Kübler-Ross, E. and Kessler, D. (2005) *On Grief and Grieving: Finding the Meaning of Grief Through the Five Stages of Loss*. New York: Scribner.

Laing, R.D. (1978) *The Politics of Experience and The Bird of Paradise*. Harmondsworth: Penguin.

Levin, J. (2001) *God, Faith, and Health: Exploring the Spirituality – Healing Connection*. New York: John Wiley and Sons.

Lin Lee, P. (2013) 'Making now precious: Working with survivors of torture and asylum seekers'. *International Journal of Narrative Therapy and Community Work 1*, 1–11.

Livingston, G., Manela, M., O'Keefe, A., Rapaport, A. et al. (2019) 'Clinical effectiveness of the START (STrAtegies for RelaTives) psychological intervention for family carers and the effects on the cost of care for people with dementia: 6-year follow-up of a randomised controlled trial'. *British Journal of Psychiatry 216*, 1, 35–42. doi:10.1192/bjp.2019.160

Macdonald, B. (1984) *Look Me in the Eye: Old Women, Aging and Ageism*. London: Women's Press.

Madsen, W.C. (2013) *Collaborative Therapy with Multi-Stressed Families*. New York: Guilford Press.

McParland, J., Flannery, H., Casdagli, L. and Portnoy, S. (2023) 'Narrative therapy approaches team away days: Creating communities'. *Clinical Child Psychology and Psychiatry 28*, 127–142.

Meehan, T. and Guilfoyle, M. (2015) 'Case formulation in poststructural narrative therapy'. *Journal of Constructivist Psychology 28*, 24–39.

Mikhailova, E. (2015) 'Application of EMDR in the treatment of older people with a history of psychical trauma'. *European Psychiatry 30*, 1, 851. doi.org/10.1016/S0924-9338(15)30664-7

Milton, S. (2017) 'What life story work means to people living with dementia'. In P. Kaiser and R. Eley (eds), *Life Story Work with People with Dementia: Ordinary Lives, Extraordinary People*. London: Jessica Kingsley Publishers.

Mitchell, G.J., Dupuis, S.L. and Kontos, P. (2013) 'Dementia discourse: From imposed suffering to knowing other-wise'. *Journal of Applied Hermeneutics*, June, Article 5, 1–19.

REFERENCES

Morgan, A. (2000) *What is Narrative Therapy? An Easy-to-Read Introduction*. Adelaide: Dulwich Centre Publications.

Morjaria-Keval, A. (2024) 'Developing collective therapeutic documents with people living alongside dementia in an NHS context'. *Faculty for the Psychology of Older People 165*, 33–40.

Murray-Parkes, C. (1972) *Bereavement: Studies of Grief in Adult Life*. London: Tavistock Institute of Human Relations.

Myerhoff, B. (1982) 'Life history among the elderly: Performance, visibility and remembering'. In J. Ruby (ed.), *A Crack in the Mirror: Reflecting Perspective in Anthropology*. Philadelphia, PA: University of Pennsylvania Press.

Myerhoff, B. (1986) 'Life not death in Venice: Its second life'. In V. Turner and E. Bruner (eds), *The Anthropology of Experience*. Chicago, IL: University of Illinois Press.

Ncube, N. (2006) 'The Tree of Life Project: Using narrative ideas in work with vulnerable children in Southern Africa'. *International Journal of Narrative Therapy and Community Work 1*, 3–16.

Ncube, N. (2007a) *Tree of Life: An Approach to Working with Vulnerable Children* [DVD]. Adelaide: Dulwich Centre Publications.

Ncube, N. (2007b) 'The Tree of Life Project'. Keynote presentation at the 8th International Conference for Narrative Therapy and Community Work, Kristiansand, Norway, 21 June 2007.

Ncube, N. (2017) *Tree of Life Practitioners Guide*. Johannesburg: Phola.

Ncube, N. and Denborough D. (2007) *Tree of Life: Mainstreaming Psychosocial Care and Support: A Manual for Facilitators*. Johannesburg: Regional Psychosocial Support Initiative.

Newman, D. (2008) '"Rescuing the said from the saying of it": Living documentation in narrative therapy'. *International Journal of Narrative Therapy and Community Work 3*, 24–34.

O'Connor, D., Sakamoto, M., Seetharaman, K., Chaudhury, H. and Phinney, A. (2022) 'Conceptualizing citizenship in dementia: A scoping review of the literature'. *Dementia 21*, 7, 2310–2350.

Offord, R. and Field, E. (2013) 'Why practitioners working in dementia should be thinking in narratives'. *FPOP Newsletter 122*, 12–16.

Oliver, K., Stembridge, L. and Lugg, A. (2022) *Forget-Me-Nots: The First Ten Years*. Canterbury, UK: Lioness Writing.

Owusu-Bempah, K. and Howitt, D. (2000) *Psychology Beyond Western Perspectives*. Leicester: BPS Books.

Ravalier, J.M., McVicar, A. and Boichat, C. (2020) 'Work stress in NHS employees: A mixed-method study'. *International Journal of Environmental Research and Public Health 17*, 18, 6464.

Reynolds, V. (2011a) 'Resisting burnout with justice-doing'. *International Journal of Narrative Therapy and Community Work 4*, 27–45.

Reynolds, V. (2011b) 'Supervision of solidarity practices: Solidarity teams and people-ing the room'. *Context 115*, 4–7.

Reynolds, V. (2012) 'An ethical stance for justice-doing in community work and therapy'. *Journal of Systemic Therapies 31*, 4, 18–33.

Reynolds, V. (2019) *Justice Doing at the Intersections of Power*. Adelaide: Dulwich Centre Publications.

Rowe, J.W. and Kahn, R.L. (1997) 'Successful aging'. *The Gerontologist 37*, 4, 433–440.

Royal College of Psychiatrists (2009) *Good Psychiatric Practice* (3rd ed.). College Report CR154. London: Royal College of Psychiatrists.

Rubinstein, R.L. and de Medeiros, K. (2015) 'Successful aging, gerontological theory and neoliberalism: A qualitative critique'. *The Gerontologist 55*, 1, 34–42.

Russell, S. and Carey, M. (2002) 'Re-membering: Responding to commonly asked questions'. *International Journal of Narrative Therapy and Community Work 3*, 23–31.

Russell, S. and Carey, M. (2004) *Narrative Therapy: Responding to Your Questions*. Adelaide: Dulwich Centre Publications.

Ryan, D. (1976) *Blaming the Victim: Defining and Defending National Interests* (Rev. ed.). New York: Random House.

Sartre, J.P. (2000) *Nausea*. London: Penguin. (Original work published 1936.)

Saunders, R., Buckman, J., Stott, J., Leibowitz, J. et al. (2021) 'Older adults respond better to psychological therapy than working-age adults: Evidence from a large sample of mental health service attendees'. *Journal of Affective Disorders 294*, 85–93. doi:10.1016/j.jad.2021.06.084

Shotter, J. (2009) 'Listening in a way that recognizes/realizes the world of "the other"'. *International Journal of Listening 23*, 1–23.

Sinden, R., Field, E. and Elias, L. (2018) 'Using Tree of Life with people with dementia living in the community'. *Faculty for the Psychology of Older People Bulletin 142*, 32–37.

Smail, D. (1978) *Psychotherapy: A Personal Approach*. London: Dent.

Smail, D. (2004) 'Therapeutic psychology and the ideology of privilege'. *Clinical Psychology 38*, 9–14.

Smail, D. (2005) *Power, Interest and Psychology: Elements of a Social Materialist Understanding of Distress*. Manchester: PCCS Books.

Smale, H. (2024) 'I was diagnosed as autistic at 39'. *BBC Radio 4: Room 5*, 1 November. www.bbc.co.uk/programmes/articles/5qDF2bM3LQpvKhpdZP5Vspr/holly-smale-i-was-diagnosed-as-autistic-at-39

Stephens, C. and Breheny, M. (2018) *Healthy Ageing: A Capability Approach to Inclusive Policy and Practice*. Abingdon and New York: Routledge.

Stephens, C., Breheny, M. and Mansvelt, J. (2015) 'Healthy ageing from the perspective of older people: A capability approach to resilience'. *Psychology & Health 30*, 6, 715–731.

Stroniska, M., Szymanski, K. and Cecchetto, V. (eds) (2014) 'Introduction: We need to talk about trauma'. In *The Unspeakable: Narratives of Trauma*. Berlin: Peter Lang.

Sweetland, J., Volmert, A.E. and O'Neil, M. (2017) *Finding the Frame*. FrameWorks Research Report.

van der Kolk, B. (2015) *The Body Keeps the Score: Brain, Mind and Body in the Healing of Trauma*: London: Penguin.

Vermeire, S. (2023) *Unravelling Trauma and Weaving Resilience with Systemic and Narrative Therapy: Playful Collaborations with Children, Families and Networks*. London: Routledge.

Weingarten, K. (2000) 'Witnessing, wonder, and hope'. *Family Process 39*, 4, 389–402.

Weingarten, K. (2003) *Common Shock: Witnessing Violence Everyday: How We Can Heal*. New York: Dutton/Penguin.

Weingarten, K. (2010) 'Reasonable hope: Construct, clinical applications, and support'. *Family Process 49*, 1, 5–25.

Weir, K. (2023) 'Ageism is one of the last socially acceptable prejudices'. *Monitor on Psychology 54*, 2. www.apa.org/monitor/2023/03/cover-new-concept-of-aging

White, C. (2009) 'Where did it all begin? Reflecting on the collaborative work of Michael White and David Epston'. *Context*, October, 59–60.

White, M. (1988) 'Saying hullo: The incorporation of the lost relationship in the resolution of grief'. *Dulwich Centre Newsletter*, spring, 29–36.

White, M. (1988/89) 'The externalising of the problem and the re-authoring of lives and relationships'. *Dulwich Centre Newsletter*, summer (special edition). (Republished in M. White, *Selected Papers*, 5–28 Adelaide: Dulwich Centre Publications, 1989.)

White, M. (1995) *Re-authoring Lives: Interviews and Essays*. Adelaide: Dulwich Centre Publications.

White, M. (1997) *Narratives of Therapists' Lives*. Adelaide: Dulwich Centre Publications.

White, M. (2000) *Reflections on Narrative Practice: Essays and Interviews*. Adelaide: Dulwich Centre Publications.

White, M. (2002) 'Journey metaphors'. *International Journal of Narrative Therapy and Community Work 4*, 12–18.

White, M. (2004a) *Narrative Practice and Exotic Lives: Resurrecting Diversity in Everyday Life*. Adelaide: Dulwich Centre Publications.

White, M. (2004b) 'Working with people who are suffering the consequences of multiple trauma: A narrative perspective'. *International Journal of Narrative Therapy and Community Work 1*, 45–76.

White, M. (2006) 'Working with people who are suffering the consequences of multiple trauma: A narrative perspective'. In D. Denborough (ed.), *Trauma: Narrative Responses to Traumatic Experience*. Adelaide: Dulwich Centre Publications.

White, M. (2007) *Maps of Narrative Practice*. New York: W.W. Norton.

White, M. and Epston, D. (1990) *Narrative Means to Therapeutic Ends*. New York: W.W. Norton.

Whyte, W. (2012) 'Passing hope around: Youth messaging strategies for becoming drug-free'. *International Journal of Narrative Therapy and Community Work 4*, 34–40.

Wingard, B. (1998) 'Introducing "sugar"'. In C. White and D. Denborough (eds), *Introducing Narrative Therapy: A Collection of Practice-Based Writings*. Adelaide: Dulwich Centre Publications.

Wingard, B. and Lester, J. (2001) *Telling Our Stories in Ways That Make Us Stronger*. Adelaide: Dulwich Centre Publications.

Worden, J.W. (1983) *Grief Counselling and Grief Therapy*. London: Tavistock.

World Health Organization (2018) *World Health Statistics 2018: Monitoring Health for the SDGs (Sustainable Development Goals)*. Geneva: WHO.

World Health Organization (2021) *Global Report on Ageism*. Geneva: WHO.

Yuen, A. (2009) 'Less pain, more gain: Explorations of responses versus effects when working with the consequences of trauma'. *Explorations: An E-Journal of Narrative Practice 1*, 1–16. www.dulwichcentre.com.au/explorations-2009-1-angel-yuen.pdf

Subject Index

ageing
    changes occurring with 81
    discourse of 43, 44–5, 58, 142
    reconceptualisation of 59
    see also narrative therapists: ageing
ageism 17, 43, 181
agency 22, 46–7, 50
ancestors, honouring 168–9
Anne 68–9
Annemarie 127, 133, 135
Arthur 67–8
Asesha
    biography 10
    distinguishing skills and ethics 157–9
    forming dementia engagement groups 126
    outsider witnessing 141, 154–5
    Tree of Life 139
    working in solidarity 21

Becky
    biography 10
    narrative maps 152–4
    'being host' 31
    burnout 69–70, 149, 164

case discussion/formulation 150–2
Chris 10, 126, 128–35, 135, 144–5, 163
club of life 37, 64–6, 168, 183
collaborative narrative practice 19
collaborative working with service users
    definitional ceremony 110–20
    letter-writing 120–2
    personal reflections of 122–3
    recommended reading 123
    setting the scene 109–10
collective documents 141, 155–7
collective narrative practice 21–2, 37–8, 125
community work *see* group and community work
connections, strengthening 141–4
context
    cultural 62–4
    locating problem in 47–50
    understanding older people in cultural, social and political 19–21
context and discourse map 50
conversations
    assisting people living with dementia and trauma 87–91
    externalising 33–6, 126
    failure 51–8
    re-authoring 36–7, 56, 73, 91
    re-membering 64–6, 67, 83–5
    spiritual 73–4
    and statement-of-position maps 33–6, 152–3
creative approaches
    creative writing 136–40
    freedom to use 184
    other 144–6
    poetry 141–4
cultural contexts 19–21, 62–4

Dan
    biography 8–9
    case discussion/formulation 150–2

Dan *cont.*
  death, dying and loss 69–72, 73
  introduction to 16
  Tree of Life 139–40
Danielle 139, 140–1
Deanne 142–4
death, dying and loss
  club of life 64–6
  cultural context 62–4
  introduction to 61–2
  re-membering practices 65–9
  spirituality 73–4
  stories responding to
    using re-membering practices 66–9
    working with groups and teams 69–72
  summary and conclusion 74–6
  supervision for support 72–3
  useful resources 76–7
de-centring 19, 31, 156
deficit discourse 43–4, 73
definitional ceremony
  bringing into practice 113
  concept of 110–11
  example of session 113–16
  experience of
    feedback from 117–18
    outsider witness responses 118–19
  setting up 119–20
  structure of session 111–12
dementia
  discourses of 125, 126, 136, 145–6
    alternative 46–7
    deficit based 43–4
  experience of, leading to lack of choice or control 22
  narrative conversations assisting people living with 87–93
  narrative practices in post-diagnostic courses 126–41
  other creative ways to support preferred identities and preferred stories 144–6
  poetry and outside witness practices 141–4
  story of, changing over time 42
  useful resources 76–7, 146–7
  see also Karen's story

Diane
  on ageing 172–3
  biography 9
  career path reflection 170–1
  future hopes and legacies 175–6
  introduction to 16
  retelling reflections 176–7
  on retirement 173–4
digital ageism 43
discourse and context map 50
discourses
  after World War II 62
  of ageing 43, 58, 142
  alternative, in relation to older people 46–7
  concept of 23
  deficit 43–4, 73
  of dementia 46–7, 125, 126, 136, 145–6
  effect of exploring 58
  and failure conversation map 51, 57
  of family 45
  of grief and loss 72
  healthy ageing 44–5
  individualism 44
  and intersectionality 45–6
  learning 101
  locating problem in 47–50
  narrative practices opening new 167
  nature of 41–2
  and power 29–30
  as 'prescriptions for living' 24, 29, 82, 182
  retirement 101, 169–70, 173, 174
  of staff burnout 69–70
  trauma 81, 84
documentation
  collective 141, 155–7
  of experience 141–4
  therapeutic 38, 70, 92
double listening 32–3, 81–2, 130

Elizabeth
  benefits of narrative therapy 19
  biography 7–8
  honouring ancestors 168
  introduction to 16, 17
  learning from older people 18
  outsider witness position 170

retelling reflections 176-8, 185
Tree of Life 126, 128, 132-3,
  135-6, 139-40, 159, 162-3
ethics, distinguishing 157-9
externalising
  conversations 33-6, 126
  as narrative therapy technique 127
  problems 34, 48, 84, 100, 153-4
  responses to trauma 85-7

failure conversations 51-8
family discourses 45
Freddi 142, 143-4

Gemma 185
  biography 8
  introduction to 16
  Tree of Life 159, 161
gender roles 100, 182
Graham's story 47-50
grief *see* death, dying and loss
Grief Legs 75-6
group and community work
  introduction to 125
  narrative practices in post-
    diagnostic courses 126-41
  other creative ways to support
    preferred identities and
    preferred stories 144-6, 184
  poetry and outside witness
    practices 141-4
  useful resources 146-7

healthy ageing discourse 44-5
Helen 185
  biography 9
  de-centred practice 19
  outsider witness questions 154
  use of definitional ceremonies
    and letter-writing 38
  working alongside service
    users 114-16, 184
host, metaphor of therapist as 31

identity 28, 44, 65-6, 160-1
  see also preferred identities
individualism 44
intersectionality 45-6

Jackie 85-7
James 118, 142, 143-4
Jane 185
  biography 9
  externalising responses
    to trauma 85-7
  outsider witnessing and collective
    documents 156-7
  re-membering conversations 83-5
  responding to loss using
    re-membering practices 67-9
  supervision 72-3, 163-4
Joan 83-5, 141
Joe 113-19, 184
June 61-2, 66-7

Karen's story
  beginning narrative therapy 96-7
  biography 9
  as carer for husband with
    dementia 22, 95
  conclusion and aftermath 107-8
  as encapsulating many issues 182
  experience of narrative
    therapy 98-101
  help from narrative therapy 101-7
  individualised course 97-8
Kate 142, 143-4
Keith 126-7, 133, 136, 144, 146, 163

letter-writing 120-2
listening
  for absent but implicit 32-3, 68,
    130
  careful 99
  double 32-3, 81-2, 130, 132
  from narrative perspective 30-1
  outsider witnesses 114-16, 120
  for 'sparkling moments' 72
Liz
  biography 9-10
  creative work 144-6
  introduction to 16
  Tree of Life 126, 136-9, 159
loss *see* death, dying and loss

Maeve's story 27, 29-30, 34-6, 38, 181
maps
  context and discourse 50

maps *cont.*
  failure conversations 51–8
  as metaphor 33
  narrative 152–4
maps *cont.*
  re-membering 65–6
  statement-of-position 33–6, 152–3
Mary 79–80, 82–3
metaphor
  dance 177
  football 114, 116
  for low mood 34
  map as 33
  moving forward 117–18
  saying goodbye/saying hullo 63
  splicing 68–9
  therapist as host 31
  Tree of Life 126, 136, 159, 180, 183
Mike 72–3
Māori proverbs 167, 180

narrative maps 152–4
narrative practice
  collaborative 19
  collective 21–2, 37–8, 125, 146
  in post-diagnostic courses for
    those with dementia 126–41
  terminology 15–16
  and trauma 81–3
  use in death, dying and loss *see*
    death, dying and loss
  see also narrative therapists;
    Tree of Life
narrative therapists
  ageing
    honouring ancestors 168–9
    introduction to 167–8
    retelling of retelling 178
    retelling reflections 176–7
    retirement discourses 169–70
    stories of future hopes
      and legacies 175–6
    stories of physical ageing 171–3
    stories of retirement 173–5
    stories of work 170–1
    summary and conclusions 178–80
    thoughts and suggestions 180
  appeal of working with
    older people 17–18

collaborative working 21–2
descriptions of stories and
  double listening 31–3
externalising conversations 33–6
introductions to 16–17
listening, being host and
  de-centring 30–1
maps as metaphor 33
passing hope around 37–8
re-authoring conversations 36–7
narrative therapy
  challenges explaining and
    describing 25–6
  'de-centred' practice in 19
  experiencing 98–101
    beginning 96–7
    benefits of 101–7
    conclusion and aftermath 107–8
    individualised course 97–8
    introduction to 95–6
  focus on strengths and
    personal agency 22–3
  identity and power 28–30
  origins 20, 26–8
  and personal contexts 19–20, 21
  recommended reading 39
  similarity to trauma-informed
    approach 21
  terminology 15–16
  use with older people having
    experienced trauma *see* trauma
  see also service users with
    narrative therapy practices,
    working alongside

older people
  appeal of working with 17–18
  discourses impacting on 43–7
  as experts in their own lives 19
  needs as under-represented
    and under-resourced 58
  understanding, in cultural, social
    and political contexts 19–21
  see also death, dying and loss;
    trauma
outsider witnesses
  and collective documents 155–7
  in definitional ceremonies 111–18
  responses 118–19

SUBJECT INDEX

setting-up 119–20
for supporting colleagues 154–8
use in facilitating conversations about end-of-life care 76–7
use in strengthening connections and documenting experiences 141–4
see also witnessing positions
outsider witness questions 127, 154, 185

Paul 121–2
personal agency 22, 46–7, 50
Pete 10
poetry
online class 145
reasons for using
fighting stigma 143–4
legacy and action 144
to strengthen connections and document experience 141–4
Polly 185
on ageing 171–2
biography 8
career attraction 21
case discussion/formulation 150–2
creative work with older people 142–3
death, dying and loss 61–2, 73–4, 75–6
future hopes and legacies 175–6
honouring ancestors 169
on inability to fool older people 19
introduction to 16, 17
learning from older people 18
retelling reflections 176–8
on retirement 173–5
spirituality 73–4
Tree of Life 139
power 27, 29–30
preferred identities
creative ways to support 144–6
failure conversations to recreate 51
letter-writing strengthening 121
losses having impact on 68
narrative questions to enrich 67
and re-authoring conversations 91
supporting through re-membering 64, 85
thickening 92, 116

re-authoring
benefits of 67–8, 69, 73
conversations 36–7, 66, 73, 91
as narrative therapy technique 127
re-membering conversations 64–6, 67, 83–5
re-membering maps 55–6
re-membering practices 64–6
honouring ancestors 171
as narrative therapy technique 127
stories of responding to loss using 66–9
retirement
dementia carer's experience of 44–5, 101–4, 108
discourses of 101, 169–70, 173, 174
psychological challenges of 44
as seen in different ways by different groups 45
stories of 173–5, 178, 184
suggestions for readers 180
Robert 121–2
Ron's story 51–8, 183
Rosslyn 185
ageing interviews 170, 172
asking the right questions 99, 182
biography 7
career attraction 18, 21
experience with dementia carer 97, 98, 99–108
future hopes and legacies interviews 175–6
honouring ancestors 168–9
introduction to 16, 17
narrative therapy with older people experiencing trauma 87–92
retelling reflections 176–8
retirement interviews 173–5
Tree of Life approach 161–2

Sara 185
benefits of narrative therapy 19
biography 8
creative work 161
therapy with older person 27, 30, 34–6, 38
service users with narrative therapy practices, working alongside
definitional ceremony 110–20

letter-writing 120–2
  personal reflections on 122–3
  recommended reading 123
  setting the scene 109–10
skills, distinguishing 157–9
social constructionism 26–7, 34
solidarity 21–2
'sparkling moments' 70, 72, 153, 178, 184
spirituality 54–5, 73–4, 183–4
standing on the riverbank 84
statement-of-position maps 33–6, 152–3
stigma
  around dementia 96–7, 125, 126, 133, 167
  challenging 23, 126, 143–4
  connected with mental health 83, 143–4, 167
  faced by people of colour 45
  psychological consequences 181
stories
  creative ways to support preferred 144–6
  definition 31
  of future hopes and legacies 175–6
  listening to 30–3
  of physical ageing 171–3
  responding to loss
    using re-membering practices 66–9
    working with groups and teams 69–72
  of retirement 173–5, 178, 184
  thin and thick descriptions of 32–3
  of work 170–1
strengths
  focus on 23
  stickperson 152
  Tree of Life trunk 131, 159
supervision 72–3, 163–4
supporting colleagues
  case discussion/formulation 150–2
  distinguishing skills and ethics 157–9
  introduction to 149–50
  narrative maps 152–4
  outsider witnessing 154–8
  summary and conclusions 164–5
  supervision 163–4
  Tree of Life 159–63
  useful resources 165

teams
  narrative practices to support 152–4
  working in 69–72
team work 69–72
therapeutic documents 38, 70, 92
Thomas's story 113–16, 184
trauma
  externalising responses to 85–7
  Mary's experience 79–80, 82–3
  narrative conversations assisting people living with 87–93
  narrative ideas about 80–1, 82
  narrative theory and practice 81–3
  re-emerging, and old age 81
  re-membering conversations 83–5
  useful resources 93–4
Tree of Life
  adaptations in creative writing groups 136–40
  celebration 127–8, 134
  Christmas 138–9
  drawing the tree 127, 128–32
  evaluation 140–1
  forest of life 127, 132–3
  as narrative practice 126
  parts of, and their representations 131, 160
  questions about professional identity 160–1
  reflections on 135–6, 180, 183
  storms, effects and responses 127, 133–4
  supporting colleagues 159–63
  tips for use of technique 129–30
  using many narrative therapy techniques 127

Val 142, 143–4
Viv's story 10, 37, 80, 88–93

The Wall 52
witnessing positions 70–1
  see also outsider witnesses

Author Index

Aman, J. 31
American Psychological Association (APA) 45
Applewhite, A. 43
Aries, P. 62
Arulampalam, S. 20

Barker, P. 63
Barrow, S. 140
Bartlett, R. 46
Beels, C. 25-6, 28
Besley, A.C. 29
Blake, D. 81, 139, 151, 152
Boichat, C. 149, 155
Bostock, J. 29
Boyle, M. 21, 83
Bredin, K. 46-7
Breheny, M. 44
Burr, V. 26, 27
Butler, R.N. 43

Cain, S. 48
Carey, M. 32-3, 64, 81-2, 158
Cecchetto, V. 80
Chaplin, R. 80
Clark, A. 63
Cohen, L. 70
Combs, G. 27, 28, 29, 30-1

Dahlin-Ivanoff, S. 50
Dalal, C. 173
Dall'Ora, C. 149
Davies, J. 44
de Medeiros, K. 44-5

Denborough, D. 21, 28, 37-8, 110, 125, 126, 159
Dupuis, S.L. 47

Eerola, P. 45
Eley, R. 92
Elias, L. 126, 130, 132, 134, 163
Epston, D. 20, 25-6, 29, 37, 110, 167, 171, 184

Felitti, V. 80
Field, E. 125, 126, 130, 132, 134, 139, 163
Foucault, M. 27, 29
Fox, H. 63-9, 70, 142, 163, 171
Fraser, J. 139
Fredman, G. 173
Freedman, J. 27, 28, 29, 30-1
Friedan, B. 175

Gergen, K.J. 44, 62, 63, 171
Goldsmith, M. 74
Greenwood, D. 48
Guilfoyle, M. 32, 150

Hayward, M. 28
Hedtke, L. 64, 171
Hensing, G. 50
Hoffman, L. 26, 31
Holland, S. 23
Holman, D. 45
Holmgren, K. 50
Horne, D. 145
Howitt, D. 20
Hughes-Roberts, J. 42

Jeffery, S. 41
Jennings, L. 144-5
Johnson, J. 140
Johnstone, L. 21, 83
Joseph Rowntree Foundation 45

Kahn, R.L. 44
Kaiser, P. 42, 62, 75-6, 81, 92, 139, 151, 152, 171
Kaseke, S. 84
Keady, J. 42
Kessler, D. 63
Kis-Sines, N. 160
Kitwood, T. 21, 46-7
Kiyimba, N. 81
Koenig, H.G. 73
Kontos, P. 47
Koppel, J. 87
Kübler-Ross, E. 62-3

Laing, R.D. 21
La Rochefoucauld, F. de 61
Larson, D.B. 73
Lester, J. 64
Levin, J. 73
Lin Lee, P. 82, 88
Livingston, G. 97
Lugg, A. 126

Macdonald, B. 43
Madsen, W.C. 44
Mansvelt, J. 44
Marie 142, 163
McCullough, M.E. 73
McParland, J. 162
McVicar, A. 149, 155
Meehan, T. 150
Mikhailova, E. 81
Milton, S. 93
Mitchell, G.J. 47
Morgan, A. 19, 31-2, 33
Morjaria-Keval, A. 141-2
Murray-Parkes, C. 63
Myerhoff, B. 64, 65, 110-11, 117

Ncube, N. 20, 126, 127, 134, 147, 159, 180

Newman, D. 92, 117

O'Connor, D. 46
Offord, R. 125
Oliver, K. 126
O'Neil, M. 59
Owusu-Bempah, K. 20

Paananen, M. 45
Pluznik, R. 160

Ravalier, J.M. 149, 155
Repo, K. 45
Reynolds, V. 70, 71, 149, 152, 154, 164, 165
Rowe, J.W. 44
Royal College of Psychiatrists 73
Rubin, D.C. 87
Rubinstein, R.L. 44-5
Russell, S. 32-3, 64, 81-2
Ryan, D. 21

Sartre, J.P. 41
Saunders, R. 43, 80
Shakespeare, W. 61
Shotter, J. 73
Sinden, R. 126, 130, 132, 134
Smail, D. 20-1, 29
Smale, H. 48-9
Stembridge, L. 126
Stephens, C. 44
Stroniska, M. 80
Sweetland, J. 59
Szymanski, K. 80

Tench, C. 142, 163

van der Kolk, B. 81
Vermeire, S. 81
Volmert, A.E. 59

Walker, A. 45
Walther, M.A. 32-3, 81-2
Weingarten, K. 70-1
Weir, K. 43
White, C. 20, 26

White, M. 20, 22, 25–6, 28, 29, 33–4, 36–7, 44, 50, 51, 63–6, 73, 81–2, 100, 110–12, 118, 119, 130, 152–3, 167–8, 171, 184
Whyte, W. 38
Williams S. 42
Wingard, B. 64, 171
Winslade, J. 64, 171
Worden, J.W. 63
World Health Organization 43

RAISING READERS
Books Build Bright Futures

Dear Reader,

We'd love your attention for one more page to tell you about the crisis in children's reading, and what we can all do.

Studies have shown that reading for fun is the **single biggest predictor of a child's future life chances** – more than family circumstance, parents' educational background or income. It improves academic results, mental health, wealth, communication skills, ambition and happiness.[1]

The number of children reading for fun is in rapid decline. Young people have a lot of competition for their time. In 2024, 1 in 10 children and young people in the UK aged 5 to 18 did not own a single book at home.[2]

Hachette works extensively with schools, libraries and literacy charities, but here are some ways we can all raise more readers:

- Reading to children for just 10 minutes a day makes a difference
- Don't give up if children aren't regular readers – there will be books for them!
- Visit bookshops and libraries to get recommendations
- Encourage them to listen to audiobooks
- Support school libraries
- Give books as gifts

There's a lot more information about how to encourage children to read on our website: **www.RaisingReaders.co.uk**

Thank you for reading.

---

1 National Literacy Trust, 'Book Ownership in 2024', November 2024, https://literacytrust.org.uk/research-services/research-reports/book-ownership-in-2024
2 OECD, '21st-Century Readers: Developing Literacy Skills in a Digital World', OECD Publishing, Paris, 2021, https://www.oecd.org/en/publications/21st-century-readers_a83d84cb-en.html